Which School?

The South-West

1995 - 96

Fourth Edition

Editor: Derek Bingham

 John Catt Educational Ltd

Published 1995 by John Catt Educational Ltd,
Great Glemham, Saxmundham, Suffolk IP17 2DH.
Tel: 01728 663666 Fax: 01728 663415

**A CIP catalogue record for this book is available from the
British Library.**

ISBN: 1-869863-79-8

ISSN: 0965-1039

Set and designed by John Catt Educational Limited,
Great Glemham, Saxmundham, Suffolk IP17 2DH.

Printed and bound in Great Britain by Bell & Bain Ltd, Glasgow.

Contents

How to use the Guide 1

Asking all the right questions, *Hilary Fender BA* 3

Finding the fees, *Anne Feek* 6

The Assisted Places Scheme 9

Reserved Entrance Awards 14

Scholarships 19

Geographical Directory of Schools
    in the South West D23

Display Listings of Schools in the South West 41

Scholarships in areas outside the South West 63

Display Listings of Schools in areas outside
    the South West 67

Directory of Tutorial Colleges and Colleges of
    Further Education D97

Display Listings of Tutorial Colleges
    and Colleges of Further Education
    in areas outside the South West 99

Educational Associations 105

Map 118

General Index 119

How to use the Guide

Wherever you live, the prospect of finding the right independent school is full of difficulties. After all, it is only when you begin your research that you can appreciate how great the choice is - and the chance of making the wrong one. And what do you do if the school you have selected is full up with a long waiting list?

In this fourth edition of **Which School? The South-West** we do two things. One is to provide as much useful advice as possible for parents. The second is to provide as much information as possible about the schools themselves.

Articles
If you turn to the contents pages you will find a list of articles. Do read them. The information they contain may save you a great deal of time. There are also lists of schools offering Reserved Entrance Awards and Assisted Places to help you.

Schools
Schools are divided into three sections. The first covers schools in Avon, Cornwall, Devon, Dorset, Somerset, and Wiltshire. They range from nursery and pre-preparatory up to sixth form day and boarding schools, boys', girls', and co-educational and are listed in alphabetical order by county.

The second includes Listings of schools outside these counties which, for various reasons such as proximity of county boundaries or ease of travel, may well attract parents.

The third section provides details of independent schools and colleges of further education, listed in alphabetical order by county.

Sections one and three are divided into two parts. The first, the Directory, contains basic information about every independent school which might come within a parent's field of choice. If an entry in the Directory is accompanied by a ★ it means that the particular school or college also appears in the Listings.

The Listings
These Listings provide schools with the opportunity to add a great deal more information about themselves than the limited space of the Directory allows. If you study them you will discover much more fully what each school has to offer.

Specialist advice
At the back of the book you will find the names and addresses of the various educational associations which can offer specialist advice. There is also a map to help locate schools.

Index
At the back is an index of all the schools which appear in the publication. The letter D preceding each page number indicates where a school appears in the

Directory. A second figure indicates where it can be found in the Listings section.

There are many ways to use this book to best advantage. If you seek schools in a certain area, look first at the appropriate Directory. It will give you the basic information about every independent school in the area.

After you have selected schools which may be suitable, look and see if they have taken a Listing. This will provide you with much more information about them before you make a direct approach.

If you know of a school, but are not sure where it is located, turn to the index. From it you will find the information you need.

Hopefully, when you have used this book you will have found a selection of suitable schools - and even options you had not been previously aware of.

Asking all the right questions

Most parents visit several schools before making the final choice for their child. Yet how many of them are really finding out what makes a school tick on those comparatively fleeting tours? It is all down to asking the right questions, says Hilary Fender, Headmistress of The Godolphin School in Salisbury.

Before you visit the school

- Ask for a prospectus, term's calendar, list of results, old newsletters and school magazines – and read them.

- If looking at a day school, make a point of going past the school as pupils arrive in the morning or leave in the afternoon. Do they look tidy, purposeful, proud to be part of the school? Do they seem friendly and well mannered, both to each other and to other passers by?

- For a day school, ask local shopkeepers what they think of the school's pupils.

When you get to the school

- Again, look at the pupils. Do they seem generally cheerful? Do they look you in the eye or do they shrink against the wall as you pass? Are they too boisterous? Would you like your child to be one of *them*?

- Look at the condition of the grounds and buildings. Are they well kept and cared for? Is there litter lying about?

- Look at the library. Is it inviting and does it appear well used? Are the computers easily accessible to pupils?

- Look at the noticeboards. Is there plenty going on? Work as well as play?

- Look at the Sixth Formers. They, after all, are the end product of the school. Do you like it?

In the Head's study

The time you spend with the Head will probably be short and invaluable. Don't waste your time asking questions that could be answered elsewhere, like how much music lessons cost or where the school uniform comes from. Concentrate instead on finding out about the person in front of you. Do their views correspond with yours? Are they a genuine reflection of the school and does the school seem to reflect their stated aims and aspirations? Do they seem really interested in their pupils and do they have a firm belief in what they – and the school – are trying to achieve? Your questions should aim to stimulate discussion, rather than yes/no answers. Ask them:

- *How well do you know your pupils and how*? Even in a large school, the Head ought to be involved with the pupils on some level (with the Sixth

Form, or the First Years, for example). Watch the Head when she is in contact with her pupils – does she have an easy relationship with them? Does she seem to like them (and they her)? Does she know their names?

- *Do you teach*? Again, it helps the Head to know her pupils and her school – and not just as a figurehead.

- *How do you recognise and deal with problems like bullying, falling in and out of friendships, petty theft, smoking*? Beware of the Head who answers this question by talking too much about the skills of her staff. You want to know how she and they cope with the children when these problems arise. Beware too of any Head who says they never do, because sometime, sooner or later, however infrequently, they will.

- *How many pupils have been expelled over the past five years and for what*? Lots of expulsions don't just mean rigorously applied discipline. They may mean that the staff lack the skill to deal with problems effectively early on, thus preventing further crises. Likewise, few expulsions are not necessarily sign of a slack regime; they are more likely to indicate a strong and purposeful school and a good team of staff who operate by common sense and thoughtfulness.

- *What happens to Upper Sixth leavers*? Be realistic – it is unlikely they are all headed for Oxbridge. Look instead for a good, broad mix of destinations and potential careers in keeping with the school's academic aims. Too many vague aspirations may indicate poor careers advice.

- *What do you look for in a teacher*? Perhaps the most important question of all. The answer should include "likes children" and "enthusiasm", because without those two qualities you cannot be a good teacher. An adage goes: ask a teacher "what do you teach?" Answer: "children" because they, not the subject, should be the important element.

- *What is the staff:pupil ratio*? But you must understand the answer. If the ratio is low, ask how staff time is used. It might, for example, mean a greater choice of GCSE or A level options, as there are enough staff to avoid timetables clashes. It may simply mean staff are given sufficient time to prepare lessons effectively.

- *What are the strengths and weaknesses of the school*? In the eyes of a pupil, a parent, the Head? A good Head should know what people think of their school, good and bad, and have reasons for the weaknesses (whether they are perceived or real) and plans to redress problems.

- *Is there any sort of child that the school DOESN'T suit*?

The moment of truth with pupils

Next you should ask to speak to a pupil. Many schools now offer 'student tours' of the school as a matter of course. Ask him or her everything you don't dare ask the Head. Pupils rarely, if ever, lie. Try:

- Do you like the Head, the staff, the food, the uniform?

- How long have you been here and are you happy? What is best about the school and what is worst?

- What sort of pupils like the school and do well?

- (For Sixth Formers) What are you and your friends going to do? Did you think about leaving to do your A levels elsewhere and, if so, what made you change your mind?

Ask to watch a lesson for a few minutes. Remember that, by the law of averages, you will probably see an average lesson. Some will be better, some worse. What is the teacher's rapport with the children? Are the pupils alert and interested?

Finance

You are quite entitled to ask about the school's finances if it is independent or grant maintained. Do so with tact and charm – you may be straying on to sensitive ground. Ask:

- Is the school in debt? If so, it will probably be serviced out of your fees.

- How are major projects financed? Is there a development or strategic plan?

Finally, don't

- Come with a checklist and spend so much time ticking it off that you fail to listen to the answers. Better to find out whether you really like the Head or not.

- Be oversharp and spend too much time trying to uncover the bad points. Schools are imperfect communities of people – and few pretend to be otherwise.

- Be so impressed by the buildings that you fail to notice the pupils.

- Bring your child with you unless you are fairly certain of your choice of school. He or she might like the pets' corner and the colour of the uniform; you might hate the Head and the academic record – and you have a family battle on your hands.

Finding the Fees

by Anne Feek, *Managing Director,*
School Fees Insurance Agency

For parents wanting the best education for their children there is one inescapable truth. The earlier the planning begins the better and advice from an independent financial adviser, with expertise in tax efficient school fees planning, should be sought as early as possible by parents who want to educate their children at an independent school.

The reasons are simple. Currently starting at around £1,000 as a day pupil at preparatory level, termly fees can rise to more than £4,000 for a boarding school. After that, because maintenance grants are means tested and those with high incomes are unlikely to qualify for support, the costs of university or further specialist training can prove equally expensive. Looked at in real terms, the first 20 years or so of a child's life can be frighteningly expensive for the parents.

But having taken the decision to pursue an education in the independent sector for their children, the question for most parents is not whether they can afford it, but how. The options fall mainly between three main methods:

> funding from capital;
>
> funding from regular savings through specialist plans;
>
> loan plans.

For those with capital, there is a variety of options including educational trusts, bonds, PEPs and unit trusts. Although they differ in style, where a predicted level of outgoings is to be met, the watch-word is generally 'the safer the better'. Of these, educational trusts are specifically designed to meet termly fees and the investment has advantageous tax treatment when the proceeds are used for educational purposes.

If the benefits under an eduational trust plan are guaranteed, the investor knows exactly what he or she is getting since the level of benefits to be provided is fixed when the investment is made and relates to the rates prevailing at the time. They have the greatest appeal for the more conservative investor – often grandparents – or for those with less than three years to run before fees are required. Generally, the plans remain extremely flexible in that benefits can be varied, postponed, brought forward or even transferred to another child.

When there are more than three years before fees are required, some educational trust plans provide greater potential for growth. With these the investment, linked to the value of units in chosen funds, will follow the fortunes of those funds up to the time when fees are required. However, investors must realise that the value of the investment can go down as well as up. It is worth noting that investment in these sorts of plans can be both from capital or by monthly payments.

The performance of the chosen funds can then be tracked by the investor, who may decide at any point in the plan's life to convert all or part of the investment to a guaranteed basis. This can be either when fees are required, or earlier if the investment conditions dictate.

A further choice for those with lump sums at their disposal are 'composition schemes' – a system of discounting fees through advanced payments – offered by some schools in the independent sector. Since there is no standard scheme or discount rate that can be quoted, it is a matter for discussing with schools direct.

Nevertheless parents should always take independent advice on this option. Amongst their considerations should be the 'return' in terms of savings on fees, how the school intends to invest the money, what the financial track record is or whether the money can be returned as a result of changes in circumstance (*eg* parent relocation, change of child's educational requirement). In general terms, however, composition schemes are of most value in the short term, particularly where there is a period of less than a year before fees are required.

For those providing school fees from regular savings, there are many choices as well as the monthly version of the educational trust plan already described. These include the familiar assortment of endowment plans, unit trusts, TESSAs and PEPs, although the last are subject to a fixed ceiling which may well be insufficient to meet projected needs.

Endowment assurance plans remain a flexible and effective means of planning from income. Careful structuring will ensure the benefits are available for fees at the right time and when not in the end used for school fees there are no tax implications. There is also the advantage of life assurance cover which can secure school fees in the event of the policy holder's death.

Where Inheritance Tax is an important consideration the policies can be written in Trust. If both parents contribute to the premiums, it is usually advisable to arrange policies on a joint life basis to ensure that benefits are paid in the event of either death. Once again it is important to remember that planning such investment calls for expert help.

The third route to education funding is for those who need to meet fees from what may appear to be inadequate resources. This situation can arise for many reasons: changes of career or of educational needs, or quite simply a peak of expenditure as more than one child needs school fees at the same time.

These are circumstances which loans of various sorts are designed to cover. The role of the schools fees specialist is not to act as lender but to conduct a 'financial health check'. Careful examination can lead to a re-structuring of commitments with the aim of making outgoings more manageable.

A mortgage may be used to provide immediate fees, or the property can be used as security to draw loans on a termly basis up to a certain amount. Unsecured loans (typically up to £15,000) can also be arranged but in nearly all cases there must be a regular premium policy in place to meet the repayments of loan and interest. Although most investors would agree that loans should be a last, rather than a first, resort there are times when a loan might just save the day.

And, whilst planning as far ahead as possible will obviously permit maximum choice in terms of investment type, even the most careful plans can be subject to change. The creation of even a small financial cushion just a few years ahead of need can provide a safety net strong enough to see parents – and their children – through.

For anyone seeking a good return on their investment, surely that is reason enough for giving at least equal consideration to financial planning as to choosing an independent school.

The Assisted Places Scheme

(Information supplied by the Department for Education)

Over 5,700 assisted places are now available each year at certain independent schools in England and Wales. They are for children who are academically able and whose parents cannot afford the full tuition fees. There is an assisted places scheme in Scotland, but with certain significant differences. Information about it can be obtained from the Scottish Education Department, Room 4/08, New St Andrew's House, Edinburgh EH1 3SY, or telephone (0131) 244 5521.

Is my child eligible for an assisted place?

The scheme is open to boys and girls. The normal age of entry is 11 or 13, but it varies from school to school.

Some assisted places are also available for pupils going straight into the sixth form.

Pupils may get assisted places at other ages, but only if they are going into a class with other pupils with assisted places who entered in a previous school year.

Pupils may get assisted places whatever type of school they have attended before. However, schools have to offer most assisted places to pupils from state schools.

To be eligible for an assisted place a pupil must have been living in the UK, the Channel Islands or the Isle of Man for two years before taking up the assisted place. A child who has been abroad for all or part of that period, (for example, if you have been working temporarily overseas), may still be eligible for a place. Special rules also apply to the children of workers from the UK and other European Union countries moving within the Union, and to refugees.

What assistance is available?

Assistance with tuition fees is available. The actual amount depends on your family income. Some families may also be eligible for help with other expenses, such as school meals and uniform and travel to and from school. More information about the help available is given below.

Under the scheme, no assistance is available with boarding fees. But if you would like your child to board, some schools which offer assisted places may themselves be willing to help with boarding fees.

What shall I have to pay towards tuition fees?

The following notes will give you an idea of whether you would qualify for assistance and how much you might have to pay.

Your contribution to fees will depend on your family's 'relevant income'.

Relevant income will normally be the total of the income (before tax) from all sources of both parents and any unearned income of all your dependent children. Then an allowance (of £1140 in 1994-95) is taken off this total for each dependent child (other than the assisted place holder) and also for each dependent relative of yours. Relevant income does not include income from child benefit, mobility allowance, some other social security benefits or scholarships or student awards.

Relevant income is normally assessed for the income tax year before the school year in question. For example, relevant income for the school year 1994-95 will be based on income in the tax year 1993-94. You will have to provide evidence of your income, such as Form P60 or a Schedule D or E tax assessment. Special rules apply if you are divorced or separated (see below); or you receive certain disability benefits; or you get income from a business with a special accounting year.

For the school year 1994-95 parents do not have to pay anything if relevant income for the tax year 1993-94 is £9352 or less. The table below gives some examples of what parents will have to pay in the school year 1994-95 if there are one or two assisted place holders in the family. This table is only a guide. The tables can be extended beyond the £25000 maximum shown. If you have three or more assisted pupils, a different scale will apply. The schools in the scheme have complete scales of contributions and will work out the amount you will have to pay. You will normally be asked to pay your share of the fees in three equal instalments, one at the start of each term.

The amount of assistance will be reviewed every year so you will have to provide details of your income again.

Parents contribution to fees: 1994-95 school year

Relevant income 1993-94 tax year (after allowances for dependents)	One assisted place holder	For each of two assisted place holders
£	£	£
9353	15	9
10000	72	54
11000	198	147
12000	348	261
13000	534	399
14000	744	558
15000	954	717
17000	1434	1077
19000	1992	1494
21000	2652	1989
23000	3312	2484
25000	3972	2979

What help is available with other expenses?

Pupils whose parents are receiving income support are eligible for free school meals. Grants of £40-£160 towards the cost of school uniform are available if your relevant income is not more than £10,462. Pupils living more than three miles from the school can get assistance with the cost of public transport. The amount will depend on your relevant income.

What happens if my income falls suddenly?

In cases of hardship - for example if income falls because a parent is out of work - your share of the fees may be worked out on current income, rather than income from a year earlier. This can be arranged in the first year your child holds an assisted place, or in later years if circumstances change.

What about divorced or separated parents?

The parents' contribution will be assessed on the relevant income of the parent who has actual custody of the child, plus the income of his or her spouse if the parent has remarried. This applies if parents are separated by a decree of judicial separation or a legal deed (or there is a court order for custody, access or maintenance, or stopping one parent from entering the matrimonial home). And it applies if they are divorced. Maintenance is included in parents' income.

How do I apply for an assisted place?

Schools choose the pupils themselves. There is only a limited number of assisted places at each school. Most schools will need your child to take an entrance exam and go on an interview. Schools' arrangements vary, so get in touch with the schools of your choice as soon as possible. They will give you all the necessary forms and information. If you have any further questions about the scheme, please contact the DFE, Assisted Places Team, Mowden Hall, Darlington, County Durham DL3 9BG; telephone 0325 392163.

Below is a list - the most up-to-date at the time of publication - of schools, by region, participating in the scheme. For each school the normal ages of entry at which assisted places are available are given: 11, 12 or 13. Sixth form entry is indicated by 'VI'. Boys' schools are shown by the letter 'B', girls' schools by 'G' and mixed schools by 'M'. Some single-sex schools have mixed entry sixth forms; these are marked '(M)'. In a few cases entry at age 11 will be to a junior department or an associated preparatory school with transfer to the main school at 13. Schools which have been authorised to offer boarding places to assisted pupils are indicated by the letter 'b'. Enquiries about boarding and about possible assistance with the boarding element of schools' fees should be addressed to the school concerned. Enquiries about assisted places at a particular school or schools should be addressed to the headmaster or headmistress.

Avon & Somerset

Bristol Cathedral School B(M) 11 & VI
Bristol Grammar School M 11 & VI
Clifton College, Bristol Mb 11
Clifton High School, Bristol Gb 11, 13 & VI
Colston's Collegiate School, Bristol Mb 11, 13 & VI
Colston's Girls' School, Bristol G 11 & VI
Queen Elizabeth's Hospital School, Clifton, Bristol Bb 11 & VI
Redland High School, Bristol G 11 & VI
The Red Maids' School, Bristol Gb 11 & VI
Bath High School G 11 & VI
King Edward's School, Bath B(M) 11, 12, 13 & VI
Kingswood School, Bath Mb 11, 12, 13 & VI
Prior Park College, Bath Mb 11
Monkton Combe School, near Bath Mb 11, 13 & VI
Wells Cathedral School Mb 11, 12, 13 & VI
Bruton School for Girls, Somerset Gb 11 & VI
King's School, Bruton B(M) 11 & 13
Taunton School Mb 11 & VI
Queen's College, Taunton Mb 11, 12, 13 & VI
Wellington School, Somerset Mb 11, 13 & VI

Devon & Cornwall

Truro High School Gb 11 & VI
Truro School Mb 11 & VI
Plymouth College B(M)b 11, 13 & VI
Exeter School B(M)b 11, 12, 13 & VI
Maynard School, Exeter G 11, 12 & VI
St Margaret's School, Exeter G 11
Edgehill College, Bideford Mb 11 & VI
West Buckland B(M)b 11, 13 & VI

Dorset & Wiltshire

Talbot Heath School, Bournemouth Gb 11, 12, 13 & VI
Canford School, Wimborne B(M)b 13 & VI
Dauntsey's School, near Devizes Mb 11
The Godolphin School, Salisbury G 11

Reserved Entrance Awards

This list is extensive, but not comprehensive, and is based upon information provided by the schools concerned. Awards which specify an academic subject (*eg* Classics), a particular locality or such like or which are reserved for the children of Old Boys or Old Girls are not listed.

For a list of schools offering Assisted Places, see page 9.

A-Art
AA-Academic ability
C-Choral
D-Drama
E-Christian Missionary or
   full-time worker
F-Her Majesty's Forces*
FO-Foreign Office
G-Games

H-Financial or domestic hardship
I-Instrumental music
M-Medical profession
O-All round ability
S-Science
T-Teaching
+-Clergy
6-VIth Form entry

* F1-The Royal Navy F2-The Royal Marines F3-The Army F4 -The Royal Air Force.

BOYS

Bramdean Grammar School, Exeter 6 I + H
Bramdean Preparatory & Grammar School, Exeter AA G I O + H
Bristol Cathedral School, Bristol 6 AA I H

Canford School, Wimborne 6 A AA I + F1 H

Downside School, Bath 6 A AA I H
Dumpton School, Wimborne A AA O + H

Exeter School, Exeter 6 AA I H

King Edward's School, Bath 6 AA H
King's Bruton Pre-Preparatory & Junior School, Yeovil O +
King's School, Bruton 6 A AA I O + H T

Milton Abbey School, Blandford Forum 6 A AA I O
Mount House School, Tavistock AA O H

The Old Malthouse, Swanage AA

The Park School, Bath AA
Plymouth College, Plymouth 6 A AA G I H

Queen Elizabeth's Hospital, Bristol 6 AA I H

Sandroyd, Salisbury H T
Sherborne School, Sherborne 6 A AA I O F

CO-EDUCATIONAL

The Abbey School, Torquay AA O
Allhallows School, Lyme Regis 6 A AA I O + F H T

Blundell's School, Tiverton 6 A AA D I O F H
Bristol Grammar School, Bristol 6 I
Bryanston School, Blandford Forum 6 A AA I H
Buckland School, Watchet I H

Castle Court Preparatory School, Wimborne AA I + E H
Chard Independent School, Chard AA
Chilton Cantelo School, Yeovil O F FO
Clayesmore Preparatory School, Blandford Forum A AA I + E F H
Clayesmore School, Blandford Forum 6 A AA G I + F H T
Clifton College, Bristol 6 A AA I O + F H T
Clifton College Preparatory School, Bristol AA G I O + F T
Colston's Collegiate School, Bristol 6 I O

Dauntsey's School, Devizes 6 A AA I O H
The Dolphin School, Exmouth O + E H
The Downs School, Bristol + F
The Duchy Grammar School, Truro 6 AA O

Edgarley Hall, Glastonbury AA I O H
Edgehill College, Bideford 6 A AA I + E F H
Exeter Cathedral School, Exeter I + H

Fairfield PNEU School, Bristol H

Gramercy Hall School, Brixham A AA I S
Grenville College, Bideford 6 A AA G I O S + F H
Grittleton House School, Chippenham AA H

The Hall School Sidcot, Winscombe AA
Homefield School, Christchurch AA I F H
Homefield School (Preparatory), Bournemouth AA I F H

The International School of Choueifat, Chippenham AA

Kelly College, Tavistock 6 A AA G I O + F H T
King's College, Taunton 6 A AA I O S + H
King's Hall School, Taunton AA G I + F
Kingswood Day Preparatory School, Bath AA I
Kingswood School, Bath 6 A AA G I + F H
Knighton House, Blandford Forum + E T

Marlborough College, Marlborough 6 A AA I O + F
Millfield School, Street 6 A AA I O S
Monkton Combe Junior School, Bath A AA G I O + E H
Monkton Combe School, Bath 6 A AA I O + E H

Newell House School, Sherborne AA + H T

The Park School, Bournemouth AA I O H
The Park School, Yeovil A AA I + E F H
Perrott Hill School, Crewkerne AA I O H
Pinewood School, Swindon + T
Polwhele House School, Truro AA I
Port Regis, Shaftesbury A AA G I O
Prior Park College, Bath 6 A AA I H

Queen's College, Taunton 6 AA I O +
Queen's College Junior School, Taunton AA I O + F H

Roselyon School, Par AA H

St Aubyns School, Tiverton AA O + E F
St John's School, Sidmouth AA F
St Martin's Independent School, Crewkerne AA H
St Martin's School, Bournemouth AA
St Michael's, Barnstaple A AA G + H
St Monica's School, Poole AA I O + F H T
St Peter's School, Exmouth AA
St Petroc's School, Bude A AA G I O F T
St Wilfrid's School, Exeter H
Salisbury Cathedral School, Salisbury AA I
Sands School, Ashburton H
Shebbear College, Beaworthy 6 A AA G O + E F H T
Sherborne Preparatory School, Sherborne AA F H
Sidcot School, Winscombe 6 AA O H

Taunton Preparatory School, Taunton A AA I O + F H T
Taunton School, Taunton 6 A AA I + E F H
Thornlow Junior School, Weymouth F
Thornlow Senior School, Weymouth F
Tockington Manor, Bristol T
Tower House School, Paignton A AA D G I O H
Treliske School, Truro AA G I O H
Tremore Christian School, Bodmin + E H
Trinity School, Teignmouth A AA D G I O + E F H
Truro School, Truro 6 A AA I F H

Warminster School, Warminster 6 AA + F H
Wellington School, Wellington 6 AA I F
Wells Cathedral Junior School, Wells I +
Wells Cathedral School, Wells 6 AA I + H

West Buckland Preparatory School, Barnstaple AA G I + F
West Buckland School, Barnstaple 6 AA I O + F H
Wolborough Hill School, Newton Abbot G I

GIRLS

Badminton School, Bristol 6 A AA D G I O S H T
Bath High School GPDST, Bath 6 AA
Bruton School for Girls, Bruton 6 AA I O

Clifton High School, Bristol 6 A AA I S H
Colston's Girls' School, Bristol H
Croft House School, Blandford Forum 6 A AA D I + F T

The Godolphin School, Salisbury 6 A AA I O H

La Retraite Leehurst School, Salisbury 6 O H
Leaden Hall, Salisbury A AA I +

The Maynard School, Exeter I H
Mount St Mary's Convent School, Exeter H

The Red Maids' School, Bristol 6 AA I
Redland High School, Bristol 6 A AA G I O S H
Rossholme School, Highbridge O H
The Royal School, Bath 6 A AA D G I O S

St Antony's-Leweston School, Sherborne 6 AA D I H
St Christopher's, Burnham-on-Sea I F H
St Dunstan's Abbey School, Plymouth 6 AA
St Joseph's School, Launceston AA H
St Margaret's Exeter, Exeter 6 AA I + H
St Mary's School, Calne A AA I + H
St Mary's School, Shaftesbury 6 A I H
St Ursula's High School, Bristol O
The School of St Clare, Penzance 6 AA I + E F H
Sherborne School for Girls, Sherborne 6 AA I H
Stonar School, Melksham 6 A AA D G I O S T
Stoodley Knowle Convent School, Torquay AA H
Stover School, Newton Abbot 6 AA I O

Talbot Heath, Bournemouth 6 AA I F H
Tremough Convent School, Penryn 6 AA I O +
Truro High School, Truro 6 AA I O +

Wentworth Milton Mount, Bournemouth 6 AA + E H
Westwing School, Bristol O F H

Scholarships

Dorset

Sherborne School for Girls

(Founded 1899)

*Sherborne,
Dorset DT9 3QN
Tel: 01935 812245 Fax: 01935 814973*

Headmistress: Miss J M Taylor, BSc, DipEd
Type: Independent Girls' Boarding School
Age range: 12-18. Boarders from 12
No. of pupils enrolled as at 1.2.95: 453
Senior: 290 Girls; Sixth Form: 163 Girls
Fees per annum:
Day: £7200; Boarding: £10,800

Religious affiliation: Church of England

Member of: GSA, BSA

Scholarships, exhibitions and bursaries:
Six academic Scholarships and two
Exhibitions are offered annually as a result
of examination and interview; in addition
there are two Scholarships offered for
outstanding promise in music. Date of
examinations: Sixth Form Scholarship in
November, others in January and February.
Winners of academic or music awards are
offered emoluments related to the current
fees.

Sherborne School for Girls is a Charitable
Trust for the purpose of educating girls in
a boarding environment.

Geographical Directory of Schools in the South West

Avon

Bath

BATH HIGH SCHOOL GPDST
Hope House, Lansdown, Bath, Avon BA1 5ES
Tel: (01225) 422931
Head: Miss M A Winfield
Type: Girls Day 4-18
No of pupils: 620
Fees: (September 94) £2808 - £3804

DOWNSIDE SCHOOL
Stratton-on-the-Fosse, Bath, Avon BA3 4RJ
Tel: (01761) 232206
Head: Rev A Bellenger
Type: Boys Boarding & Day 10-18
No of pupils: 420 No of Boarders F400
Fees: (September 94) FB £8694 - £10836 DAY £6159 - £6945

KING EDWARD'S JUNIOR SCHOOL
North Road, Bath, Avon BA2 6JA
Tel: (01225) 463218
Head: P M Garner
Type: Boys Day 7-11
No of pupils: 179
Fees: (September 94) £2919

KING EDWARD'S SCHOOL, BATH
North Road, Bath, Avon BA2 6HU
Tel: (01225) 464313
Head: P J Winter
Type: Boys Day 7-18 (Co-ed VIth form)
No of pupils: B643 G47
Fees: (September 94) £2919 - £4056

KINGSWOOD DAY PREPARATORY SCHOOL
Hermitage House, 4-5 Portland Place, Bath, Avon BA1 2RU
Tel: (01225) 310468
Head: Mrs M H Newbery
Type: Co-educational Day 3-11
No of pupils: B46 G55
Fees: (September 94) £1282 - £3150

KINGSWOOD SCHOOL
Lansdown, Bath, Avon BA1 5RG
Tel: (01225) 311627
Head: G M Best
Type: Co-educational Boarding & Day 11-18
No of pupils: B255 G190 No of Boarders F220 W29
Fees: (September 94) F/WB £8415 - £10680 DAY £5325 - £6810

MONKTON COMBE JUNIOR SCHOOL
Combe Down, Bath, Avon BA2 7ET
Tel: (01225) 837912
Head: E J Clarke
Type: Co-educational Day & Boarding 3-13
No of pupils: B211 G28 No of Boarders F61
Fees: (September 94) FB £8385 DAY £1785 - £5925

MONKTON COMBE SCHOOL
Bath, Avon BA2 7HG
Tel: (01225) 721102
Head: M J Cuthbertson
Type: Co-educational Boarding & Day 11-18
No of pupils: B218 G104 No of Boarders F274
Fees: (September 94) FB £9330 - £11280
DAY £6450 - £7830

PARAGON SCHOOL
Lyncombe House, Lyncombe Vale, Bath, Avon BA2 4LT
Tel: (01225) 310837
Head: D J Martin
Type: Co-educational Day 3-11
No of pupils: B135 G133
Fees: (September 94) £2370 - £2640

THE PARK SCHOOL
Weston Lane, Bath, Avon BA1 4AQ
Tel: (01225) 421681
Head: R E Chambers
Type: Boys Day 3-11 (Girls nursery only)
No of pupils: 140
Fees: (September 94) £2520 - £3810

PRIOR PARK COLLEGE
Bath, Avon BA2 5AH
Tel: (01225) 835353
Head: J W Goulding
Type: Co-educational Boarding & Day 11-18
No of pupils: B271 G192 No of Boarders F171 W21
Fees: (September 94) F/WB £9696 DAY £5133 - £5361

★ THE ROYAL SCHOOL
Lansdown, Bath, Avon BA1 5SZ
Tel: (01225) 313877
Head: Mrs E McKendrick
Type: Girls Boarding & Day 3-18 (Boys 3-7)
No of pupils: B12 G320 No of Boarders F241
Fees: (September 94) FB £8991 - £10680
DAY £2781 - £5886

Bristol

AMBERLEY HOUSE SCHOOL
42 Apsley Road, Clifton, Bristol, Avon BS8 2SU
Tel: (0117) 973 5515
Head: Mrs H Tallis
Type: Co-educational Day 2-11
No of pupils: B100 G70
Fees: (September 94) £710 - £2130

★ BADMINTON SCHOOL
Westbury-on-Trym, Bristol, Avon BS9 3BA
Tel: (0117) 9623141
Head: C J T Gould
Type: Girls Boarding & Day 5-18
No of pupils: 360 No of Boarders F230
Fees: (September 94) FB £7995 - £10725
DAY £2850 - £5925

BRISTOL CATHEDRAL SCHOOL
College Square, Bristol, Avon BS1 5TS
Tel: (0117) 929 1872
Head: K J Riley
Type: Boys Day 10-18 (Co-ed VIth form)
No of pupils: B435 G25
Fees: (September 94) £3903

★ **BRISTOL GRAMMAR SCHOOL**
University Road, Bristol, Avon BS8 1SR
Tel: (01179) 736006
Head: C E Martin (Lower School: Mrs J Jenkins)
Type: Co-educational Day 7-18
No of pupils: B822 G399
Fees: (September 94) £2205 - £3705

BRISTOL WALDORF SCHOOL
Park Place, Clifton, Bristol, Avon BS8 1JR
Tel: (0117) 926 0440
Type: Co-educational Day 3-14
No of pupils: 263
Fees: On application

CLEVE HOUSE SCHOOL
254 Wells Road, Bristol, Avon BS4 2PN
Tel: (0117) 977 7218
Heads: D La and Mrs E Lawson
Type: Co-educational Day 2-11
No of pupils: B115 G95
Fees: (September 94) £1950 - £2085

CLIFTON COLLEGE
32 College Road, Bristol, Avon BS8 3JH
Tel: (0117) 973 9187
Head: A H Monro
Type: Co-educational Boarding & Day 13-18
No of pupils: B500 G150 No of Boarders F390
Fees: (September 94) FB £11685 DAY £8190

CLIFTON COLLEGE PREPARATORY SCHOOL
The Avenue, Clifton, Bristol, Avon BS8 3HE
Tel: (0117) 973 7264
Head: Dr R J Acheson
Type: Co-educational Boarding & Day 3-13
No of pupils: B370 G100 No of Boarders F90 W20
Fees: (September 94) FB £8487 WB £8178
DAY £1230 - £6135

★ **CLIFTON HIGH SCHOOL**
College Road, Clifton, Bristol, Avon BS8 3JD
Tel: (0117) 973 0201
Head: Mrs J D Walters
Type: Girls Day 3-18 (Boarders 16-18, day boys 3-11)
No of pupils: B73 G677 No of Boarders F28 W6
Fees: (September 94) FB £7935 - £8655 WB £7530 - £8220
DAY £780 - £4575

COLSTON'S COLLEGIATE SCHOOL
Stapleton, Bristol, Avon BS16 1BJ
Tel: (0117) 965 5207
Head: S B Howarth
Type: Co-educational Boarding & Day 3-18
No of pupils: B453 G99 No of Boarders F72
Fees: (September 94) FB £7290 - £9516 WB £6990 - £9060
DAY £3810 - £5400

COLSTON'S GIRLS' SCHOOL
Cheltenham Road, Bristol, Avon BS6 5RD
Tel: (0117) 942 4328
Head: Mrs J P Franklin
Type: Girls Day 10-18
No of pupils: 550
Fees: (September 94) £3402

THE DOWNS SCHOOL
Wraxall, Bristol, Avon BS19 1PF
Tel: (01275) 852008
Head: J K Macpherson
Type: Co-educational Boarding & Day 3-13
No of pupils: B250 G50 No of Boarders F60
Fees: (September 94) F/WB £6810 DAY £1590 - £4905

FAIRFIELD PNEU SCHOOL
Fairfield Way, Farleigh Road, Backwell, Bristol,
Avon BS19 3PD
Tel: (01275) 462743
Head: Mrs A Nosowska
Type: Co-educational Day 3-11
No of pupils: B53 G63
Fees: (September 94) £1020 - £3120

GRACEFIELD PREPARATORY SCHOOL
266 Overndale Road, Fishponds, Bristol, Avon BS16 2RG
Tel: (0117) 956 7977
Head: Mrs M Garman
Type: Co-educational Day 4-11
No of pupils: B45 G45
Fees: (September 94) £1614 - £1785

OAK HILL SCHOOL
Okebourne Road, Brentry, Bristol, Avon BS10 6QY
Tel: (0117) 959 1083
Head: Mrs H Jelfs
Type: Co-educational Day 4-11
No of pupils: 90
Fees: On application

OVERNDALE SCHOOL
Chapel Lane, Old Sodbury, Bristol, Avon BS17 6NQ
Tel: (01454) 310332
Head: M R Wallis-Eade
Type: Co-educational Day 3-11
No of pupils: B55 G45
Fees: (September 94) £1860

QUEEN ELIZABETH'S HOSPITAL
Berkeley Place, Clifton, Bristol, Avon BS8 1JX
Tel: (0117) 929 1856
Head: Dr R Gliddon
Type: Boys Day & Boarding 11-18
No of pupils: 500 No of Boarders F90
Fees: (September 94) FB £6544 DAY £3727

THE RED MAIDS' SCHOOL
Westbury-on-Trym, Bristol, Avon BS9 3AW
Tel: (0117) 962 2641
Head: Miss S Hampton
Type: Girls Boarding & Day 11-18
No of pupils: 500 No of Boarders F100
Fees: (September 94) FB £7200 DAY £3630

★ **REDLAND HIGH SCHOOL**
Redland Court, Redland, Bristol, Avon BS6 7EF
Tel: (0117) 9245796
Head: Mrs C Lear
Type: Girls Day 4-18
No of pupils: 640
Fees: (September 94) £2451 - £3777

SACRED HEART PREPARATORY SCHOOL
Chew Magna, Bristol, Avon BS18 8PT
Tel: (0117) 933 2470
Head: Ms V Kavanagh
Type: Co-educational Day 3-11
No of pupils: 147
Fees: (September 94) £1800

ST URSULA'S HIGH SCHOOL
Brecon Road, Westbury-on-Trym, Bristol,
Avon BS9 4DT
Tel: (0117) 962 2616
Head: Mrs M A Macnaughton
Type: Girls Day 3-18 (Boys 3-11)
No of pupils: B69 G350
Fees: (September 94) £945 - £2985

SILVERHILL SCHOOL
Swan Lane, Winterbourne, Bristol, Avon BS17 1RL
Tel: (01454) 772156
Heads: Mr & Mrs G J Clewer
Type: Co-educational Day 2-13
No of pupils: B164 G142
Fees: (September 94) £1920 - £3243

TOCKINGTON MANOR
Tockington, Bristol, Avon BS12 4NY
Tel: (01454) 613229
Head: R G Tovey
Type: Co-educational Day & Boarding 3-14
No of pupils: B100 G60 No of Boarders F50
Fees: (September 94) FB £8385 DAY £1155 - £5850

TORWOOD HOUSE SCHOOL
29 Durdham Park, Redland, Bristol, Avon BS6 6XE
Tel: (0117) 973 5620
Head: Mrs S Sheppard
Type: Co-educational Day 2-11
No of pupils: 190
Fees: (September 94) £560 - £2100

WESTWING SCHOOL
Kyneton House, Thornbury, Bristol, Avon BS12 2JZ
Tel: (01454) 412311
Head: Mrs A Rispin
Type: Girls Boarding & Day 4-18
No of pupils: 110 No of Boarders F60 W10
Fees: (September 94) FB £7242 - £7650 WB £7005 - £7440
DAY £1980 - £3690

Clevedon

RYDAL PRE-PREPARATORY SCHOOL
11 Albert Road, Clevedon, Avon BS21 7RP
Tel: (01275) 874127
Head: Mrs E A Humby
Type: Co-educational Day 4-11
No of pupils: B15 G15
Fees: (September 94) £2100

ST BRANDON'S SCHOOL
Elton Road, Clevedon, Avon BS21 7SD
Tel: (01275) 875092
Head: Mrs S Vesey
Type: Co-educational Day 3-13
No of pupils: 125
Fees: (September 94) £1350 - £2685

Weston-Super-Mare

ASHBROOKE HOUSE
9 Ellenborough Park North, Weston-Super-Mare, Avon BS23 1XH
Tel: (01934) 629515
Head: J C Teasdale
Type: Co-educational Day 3-11
No of pupils: B50 G15
Fees: (September 94) £1365 - £1833

LANCASTER HOUSE SCHOOL
38 Hill Road, Weston-Super-Mare, Avon BS23 2RY
Tel: (01934) 624116
Head: Mrs S Lewis
Type: Co-educational Day 4-11
No of pupils: B30 G40
Fees: (September 94) £960 - £1020

WYNCROFT
5 Charlton Road, Weston-Super-Mare, Avon
Tel: (01934) 626556
Head: Mrs E M Thorn
Type: Co-educational Day 4-11
No of pupils: 100
Fees: On application

Winscombe

★ **THE HALL SCHOOL**
(PRE-PREPARATORY SCHOOL FOR SIDCOT)
Winscombe, Avon BS25 1PD
Tel: (01934) 844118
Head: Mrs W Wardman
Type: Co-educational Day 3-8
No of pupils: B32 G24
Fees: (September 94) £1425 - £2790

SIDCOT SCHOOL
Winscombe, Avon BS25 1PD
Tel: (01934) 843102
Head: C Greenfield
Type: Co-educational Boarding & Day 9-18
No of pupils: B198 G177 No of Boarders F175
Fees: (September 94) F/WB £9282 DAY £4104 - £5550

Cornwall

Bodmin

TREMORE CHRISTIAN SCHOOL
Tremore Manor, Lanivet, Bodmin, Cornwall PL30 5JT
Tel: (01208) 831713
Head: Miss A Whitaker
Type: Co-educational Day 3-16
No of pupils: B19 G19
Fees: On application

Bude

ST PETROC'S SCHOOL
Ocean View Road, Bude, Cornwall EX23 8NJ
Tel: (01288) 352876
Head: M J Glen
Type: Co-educational Boarding & Day 3-13
No of pupils: B62 G45 No of Boarders F17 W7
Fees: (September 94) FB £6115 WB £5742
DAY £2284 - £3816

Launceston

ST JOSEPH'S SCHOOL
15 St Stephen's Hill, Launceston, Cornwall PL15 8HN
Tel: (01566) 772988
Head: A G Taylor
Type: Girls Day & Boarding 4-16 (Boys 4-11)
No of pupils: B35 G186 No of Boarders F2 W27
Fees: (September 94) FB £6264 - £6840 WB £5124 - £5814
DAY £2209 - £3129

Par

ROSELYON SCHOOL
St Blazey Road, Par, Cornwall PL24 2HZ
Tel: (01726) 812110
Head: A J Stone
Type: Co-educational Day 3-11
No of pupils: B50 G50
Fees: (September 94) £783 - £2610

Penryn

TREMOUGH CONVENT SCHOOL
Penryn, Cornwall TR10 9EZ
Tel: (01326) 372226
Head: Sr Maria
Type: Girls Boarding & Day 3-18 (Boys 3-11)
No of pupils: B20 G240 No of Boarders W56
Fees: (September 94) WB £4500 DAY £2700 - £2850

Penzance

THE SCHOOL OF ST CLARE
Polwithen, Penzance, Cornwall TR18 4JR
Tel: (01736) 63271
Head: I Halford
Type: Girls Boarding & Day 3-18 (Boys 3-11)
No of pupils: B35 G160 No of Boarders F33 W11
Fees: (September 94) FB £7590 - £7965 WB £7281 - £7500
DAY £1005 - £4260

Truro

THE DUCHY GRAMMAR SCHOOL
Tregye, Carnon Downs, Truro, Cornwall TR3 6JH
Tel: (01872) 862289
Head: M L Fuller
Type: Co-educational Day & Boarding 3-18
No of pupils: B100 G40 No of Boarders F25 W20
Fees: (September 94) FB £6972 - £7782 WB £6708 - £7518
DAY £2541 - £4170

POLWHELE HOUSE SCHOOL
Newquay Road, Truro, Cornwall TR4 9AE
Tel: (01872) 73011
Heads: Mr and Mrs R I White
Type: Co-educational Day & Boarding 3-13
No of pupils: B127 G93 No of Boarders W18
Fees: (September 94) WB £7425 - £7665 DAY £480 - £4320

TRELISKE SCHOOL
Truro, Cornwall TR1 3QN
Tel: (01872) 72616
Head: R L Hollins
Type: Co-educational Day & Boarding 3-11
No of pupils: B150 G60 No of Boarders F20
Fees: (September 94) FB £7197 DAY £2649 - £4038

TRESCOL VEAN SCHOOL
Baldhu, Truro, Cornwall TR3 6EG
Tel: (01872) 560788
Head: Mrs S M Baron
Type: Co-educational Day 3-7
No of pupils: B36 G36
Fees: (September 94) £702 - £2340

TRURO HIGH SCHOOL
Falmouth Road, Truro, Cornwall TR1 2HU
Tel: (01872) 72830
Head: J Graham Brown
Type: Girls Boarding & Day 3-18 (Boys 3-5)
No of pupils: 400 No of Boarders F46 W42
Fees: (September 94) FB £7395 - £7695 WB £7296 - £7596
DAY £3915 - £4215

TRURO SCHOOL
Trennick Lane, Truro, Cornwall TR1 1TH
Tel: (01872) 72763
Head: G A Dodd
Type: Co-educational Day & Boarding 11-18
No of pupils: B601 G236 No of Boarders F178
Fees: (September 94) F/WB £7197 - £8259 DAY £4038 - £4434

Devon

Ashburton

★ **SANDS SCHOOL**
Greylands, 48 East Street, Ashburton, Devon TQ13 7AX
Tel: (01364) 53666
Head: S Bellamy
Type: Co-educational Day 10-18
No of pupils: B24 G16
Fees: (September 94) £2970 - £3045

Barnstaple

★ **ST MICHAEL'S**
Tawstock Court, Barnstaple, Devon EX31 3HY
Tel: (01271) 43242
Head: R K Yetzes
Type: Co-educational Boarding & Day 3-13
No of pupils: B131 G76 No of Boarders F50
Fees: (September 94) FB £5250 - £7620 WB £5250 - £7230
DAY £2340 - £4695

WEST BUCKLAND PREPARATORY SCHOOL
Langholme, West Buckland, Barnstaple, Devon EX32 0SX
Tel: (01598) 760545
Head: G D Benfield
Type: Co-educational Day & Boarding 5-11
No of pupils: B63 G31 No of Boarders F17
Fees: (September 94) FB £6570 - £7710 DAY £2385 - £4215

WEST BUCKLAND SCHOOL
Barnstaple, Devon EX32 0SX
Tel: (01598) 760281
Head: M Downward
Type: Co-educational Boarding & Day 11-18
No of pupils: B279 G180 No of Boarders F145
Fees: (September 94) FB £8544 DAY £4635

Beaworthy

SHEBBEAR COLLEGE
Shebbear, Beaworthy, Devon EX21 5HJ
Tel: (01409) 281228
Head: R J Buley
Type: Co-educational Boarding & Day 3-18
No of pupils: 290
Fees: (September 93) FB £5250 - £8460 DAY £2550 - £4620

Bideford

EDGEHILL COLLEGE
Northdown Road, Bideford, Devon EX39 3LY
Tel: (01237) 471701
Head: Mrs E M Burton
Type: Co-educational Boarding & Day 3-19
No of pupils: B86 G430 No of Boarders F110 W33
Fees: (September 94) FB £6480 - £9030 WB £5850 - £8160
DAY £2385 - £4965

GRENVILLE COLLEGE
Bideford, Devon EX39 3JR
Tel: (01237) 472212
Head: Dr M C Cane
Type: Co-educational Boarding & Day 3-18 (Boarders from 11)
No of pupils: B300 G240 No of Boarders F150
Fees: (September 94) FB £9348 - £9480
DAY £1785 - £4650

SMALL SCHOOL
Fore Street, Hartland, Bideford, Devon EX39 6AB
Tel: (01237) 441672
Head: R Secombe
Type: Co-educational Day 11-16
No of pupils: 40
Fees: On application

Brixham

GRAMERCY HALL SCHOOL
Churston Ferrers, Brixham, Devon TQ5 0HR
Tel: (01803) 844338
Head: R Purdom
Type: Co-educational Day 3-16
No of pupils: B85 G45
Fees: (September 94) £1200 - £3885

Crediton

SHOBROOKE HOUSE SCHOOL
Shobrooke, Crediton, Devon EX17 1AP
Tel: (01363) 22715
Head: P G Spencer
Type: Co-educational Day 3-11
No of pupils: B32 G28
Fees: (September 94) £630 - £1860

Dawlish

LANHERNE SCHOOL
18 Longlands, Dawlish, Devon EX7 9NG
Tel: (01626) 863091
Head: Mrs P Robins
Type: Co-educational Day 2-8
No of pupils: 60
Fees: (September 94) £1050 - £1500

Exeter

BENDARROCH SCHOOL
Aylesbeare, Exeter, Devon EX5 2BY
Tel: (01395) 233553
Head: N R Home
Type: Co-educational Day 5-13
No of pupils: B20 G20
Fees: (September 94) £2175 - £2565

BRAMDEAN GRAMMAR SCHOOL
Richmond Lodge, Homefield Road, Heavitree, Exeter,
Devon EX1 2QR
Tel: (01392) 73387
Head: D A Connett
Type: Boys Boarding & Day 11-17 (Co-ed VIth form)
No of pupils: 180 No of Boarders W25
Fees: (September 94) WB £1990 - £5478
DAY £1264 - £3480

BRAMDEAN PREPARATORY & GRAMMAR SCHOOL
Richmond Lodge, Homefield Road, Heavitree, Exeter,
Devon EX1 2QR
Tel: (01392) 73387
Head: D Stoneman
Type: Boys Boarding & Day 7-11
No of pupils: B140 G6 No of Boarders W20
Fees: (September 94) WB £5970 DAY £3792

ELM GROVE SCHOOL
Elm Grove Road, Topsham, Exeter, Devon EX3 0EQ
Tel: (01392) 873031
Heads: B E & Mrs K M Parsons
Type: Co-educational Day 3-7
No of pupils: B30 G30
Fees: (September 94) £1650

EXETER CATHEDRAL SCHOOL
The Chantry, Palace Gate, Exeter, Devon EX1 1HX
Tel: (01392) 55298
Head: R A Hay
Type: Co-educational Day & Boarding 4-13
No of pupils: 133 No of Boarders F26 W4
Fees: (September 94) FB £6645 WB £6615
DAY £2265 - £4095

EXETER PREPARATORY SCHOOL
Victoria Park Road, Exeter, Devon EX2 4NS
Tel: (01392) 58712
Head: J B Lawford
Type: Boys Day 7-11
No of pupils: 100
Fees: (September 94) £3390 - £3685

EXETER SCHOOL
Exeter, Devon EX2 4NS
Tel: (01392) 73679
Head: N W Gamble
Type: Boys Boarding & Day 11-18 (Co-ed VIth form)
No of pupils: B657 G48 No of Boarders F60
Fees: (September 94) F/WB £7452 DAY £2390 - £3942

HYLTON KINDERGARTEN & PRE-PREPARATORY SCHOOL
13A Lyndhurst Road, Exeter, Devon EX2 4PA
Tel: (01392) 54755
Head: Mrs B J Glass
Type: Co-educational Day 4-8
No of pupils: 60
Fees: (September 94) £1500 - £2142

THE MAYNARD SCHOOL
Denmark Road, Exeter, Devon EX1 1SJ
Tel: (01392) 73417
Head: Miss F Murdin
Type: Girls Day 7-18
No of pupils: 560
Fees: (September 94) £3120 - £3900

★ **MOUNT ST MARY'S CONVENT SCHOOL**
Wonford Road, Exeter, Devon EX2 4PF
Tel: (01392) 436770
Head: Sr Eileen Delaney
Type: Girls Day 3-18 (Boys 3-7)
No of pupils: 450
Fees: (September 94) £2400 - £3285

ST MARGARET'S EXETER
Magdalen Road, Exeter, Devon EX2 4TS
Tel: (01392) 73197
Head: Mrs M D'Albertanson
Type: Girls Day 5-18
No of pupils: 440
Fees: (September 94) £2625 - £3810

ST WILFRID'S SCHOOL
25 St David's Hill, Exeter, Devon EX4 4DA
Tel: (01392) 76171
Head: J G Bushrod
Type: Co-educational Day 3-16
Fees: (September 94) £1770 - £2835

Exmouth

THE DOLPHIN SCHOOL
Raddenstile Lane, Exmouth, Devon EX8 2JH
Tel: (01395) 272418
Head: R J Higgins
Type: Co-educational Day 3-13
No of pupils: 60
Fees: (September 94) £1920

ST PETER'S SCHOOL
Harefield, Lympstone, Exmouth, Devon EX8 5AU
Tel: (01395) 272148
Head: C N Abram
Type: Co-educational Day & Boarding 5-13
No of pupils: B140 G57 No of Boarders W40
Fees: (September 94) WB £5985 DAY £2925 - £4170

Honiton

MANOR HOUSE SCHOOL
Springfield House, Honiton, Devon EX14 8TL
Tel: (01404) 42026
Head: P A Eyles
Type: Co-educational Boarding & Day 3-13
No of pupils: B100 G80 No of Boarders W12
Fees: (September 94) WB £4620 DAY £2085 - £2670

Kingsbridge

KINGSBRIDGE PREPARATORY SCHOOL
The Gatehouse, Embankment Road, Kingsbridge,
Devon TQ7 1JN
Tel: (01548) 852703
Head: Mrs J C Johnson
Type: Co-educational Day 2-11
No of pupils: 60
Fees: (September 94) £2775 - £2970

Newton Abbot

★ **ST BERNARD'S PREPARATORY SCHOOL**
9 Courtenay Road, Newton Abbot, Devon TQ12 1HP
Tel: (01626) 65424
Head: R Dudley-Cooke
Type: Co-educational Day 2-11
No of pupils: B35 G65
Fees: (September 93) £720 - £2574

STOVER SCHOOL
Newton Abbot, Devon TQ12 6QG
Tel: (01626) 54505
Head: Mrs W E Lunel
Type: Girls Boarding & Day 11-18
No of pupils: 250 No of Boarders F62 W80
Fees: (September 94) FB £7920 WB £7725 DAY £4158

WOLBOROUGH HILL SCHOOL
South Road, Newton Abbot, Devon TQ12 1HH
Tel: (01626) 54078
Head: S J Day
Type: Co-educational Day & Boarding 4-13
No of pupils: B202 G32 No of Boarders W29
Fees: (September 94) WB £6330 DAY £4350

Paignton

GREYLANDS SCHOOL
9 Belle Vue Road, Paignton, Devon TQ4 6ES
Tel: (01803) 557298
Head: Mrs P M Adams
Type: Co-educational Day 3-11
No of pupils: 100
Fees: (September 94) £1680 - £1935

TOWER HOUSE SCHOOL
Fisher Street, Paignton, Devon TQ4 5EW
Tel: (01803) 557077
Head: M Robinson
Type: Co-educational Day 3-16
No of pupils: B93 G85
Fees: (September 94) £2445 - £3735

Plymouth

FLETEWOOD SCHOOL
88 North Road East, Plymouth, Devon PL4 6AN
Tel: (01752) 663782
Head: J Martin
Type: Co-educational Day 3-11
No of pupils: B35 G35
Fees: (September 94) £1500

KING'S SCHOOL
Hartley Road, Plymouth, Devon PL3 5LW
Tel: (01752) 771789
Head: Mrs J Lee
Type: Co-educational Day 3-11
No of pupils: B58 G73
Fees: (September 94) £1650 - £1995

PLYMOUTH COLLEGE
Ford Park, Plymouth, Devon PL4 6RN
Tel: (01752) 228596
Head: A J Morsley
Type: Boys Day & Boarding 11-18 (Co-ed VIth form)
No of pupils: B580 G40 No of Boarders F40 W49
Fees: (September 94) FB £8282 WB £8232 DAY £4326

PLYMOUTH COLLEGE PREPARATORY SCHOOL
Hartley Road, Plymouth, Devon PL3 5LW
Tel: (01752) 772283
Head: G Pessell
Type: Co-educational Day 4-11
No of pupils: B244 G6
Fees: (September 94) £2226 - £3180

ST DUNSTAN'S ABBEY PREPARATORY SCHOOL
North Road West, Plymouth, Devon PL1 5DH
Tel: (01752) 226153
Head: Mrs A J Bailey
Type: Girls Day & Boarding 4-11 (Boys 4-7)
No of pupils: 110 No of Boarders W5
Fees: (September 94) WB £2460 DAY £2283 - £2910

ST DUNSTAN'S ABBEY SCHOOL
North Road West, Plymouth, Devon PL1 5DH
Tel: (01752) 663998
Head: R A Bye
Type: Girls Day & Boarding 11-18
No of pupils: 363 No of Boarders W39
Fees: (September 94) WB £5370 - £6750 DAY £2280 - £4290

WESTERN COLLEGE PREPARATORY SCHOOL
Seymour Road, Mannamead, Plymouth, Devon PL3 5AS
Tel: (01752) 668558
Head: Mrs M A Knaggs
Type: Girls Day 4-11
No of pupils: 120
Fees: (September 94) £2025 - £2190

Seaton

WHITE HOUSE SCHOOL
Old Beer Road, Seaton, Devon EX12 2PX
Tel: (01297) 20614
Head: H R Doran
Type: Co-educational Day 4-13
No of pupils: B50 G44
Fees: (September 94) £1615 - £2025

Sidmouth

ST JOHN'S SCHOOL
Broadway, Sidmouth, Devon EX10 8RG
Tel: (01395) 513984
Head: N R Pockett
Type: Co-educational Day & Boarding 3-13
No of pupils: B140 G128 No of Boarders F70 W35
Fees: (September 94) F/WB £5985 DAY £2100 - £3555

Tavistock

KELLY COLLEGE
Tavistock, Devon PL19 0HZ
Tel: (01822) 612010
Head: C H Hirst
Type: Co-educational Boarding & Day 11-18
No of pupils: B241 G62 No of Boarders F122 W46
Fees: (September 94) FB £10950 WB £10485
DAY £4785 - £6750

KELLY COLLEGE JUNIOR SCHOOL - ST MICHAEL'S
Hazeldon House, Parkwood Road, Tavistock,
Devon PL19 0JS
Tel: (01822) 612919
Head: M J Nicholls
Type: Co-educational Day 4-11
No of pupils: B45 G55
Fees: (September 94) £2430 - £2985

MOUNT HOUSE SCHOOL
Tavistock, Devon PL19 9JL
Tel: (01822) 612244
Head: C D Price
Type: Boys Boarding & Day 7-14
No of pupils: 170 No of Boarders F150
Fees: (September 94) FB £7854 DAY £5694

Teignmouth

★ TRINITY SCHOOL
Buckeridge Road, Teignmouth, Devon TQ14 8LY
Tel: (01626) 774138
Head: C J Ashby
Type: Co-educational Day & Boarding 3-18
No of pupils: B159 G142 No of Boarders F54 W4
Fees: (September 94) FB £7050 - £7800 WB £6848 - £7598
DAY £2460 - £3930

Tiverton

BLUNDELL'S SCHOOL
Tiverton, Devon EX16 4DN
Tel: (01884) 252543
Head: J Leigh
Type: Co-educational Boarding & Day 13-18
No of pupils: B375 G48 No of Boarders F330
Fees: (September 94) FB £11145 DAY £6795

ST AUBYNS SCHOOL
Howden Court, Tiverton, Devon EX16 5PB
Tel: (01884) 252393
Head: A C Herniman
Type: Co-educational Day & Boarding 3-13
No of pupils: B175 G102 No of Boarders F22 W12
Fees: (September 94) F/WB £5661 - £6567 DAY £504 - £4152

Torquay

THE ABBEY SCHOOL
Hampton Court, St Marychurch, Torquay, Devon TQ1 4PR
Tel: (01803) 327868
Head: Mrs S J Greinig
Type: Co-educational Day 2-11
No of pupils: B110 G110
Fees: (September 94) £300 - £2850

STOODLEY KNOWLE CONVENT SCHOOL
Ansteys Cove Road, Torquay, Devon TQ1 2JB
Tel: (01803) 293160
Head: Sr Perpetua
Type: Girls Boarding & Day 5-18
No of pupils: 200 No of Boarders W70
Fees: (September 94) WB £3750 - £4242 DAY £2100 - £2640

Totnes

RUDOLF STEINER SCHOOL
Hood Manor, Buckfastleigh Road, Dartington, Totnes,
Devon TQ9 6AB
Tel: (01803) 762 528
Head: C R Cooper
Type: Co-educational Day 3-16
No of pupils: B114 G122
Fees: (September 94) £1244 - £2378

Dorset

Blandford Forum

BRYANSTON SCHOOL
Blandford Forum, Dorset DT11 0PX
Tel: (01258) 452411
Head: T D Wheare
Type: Co-educational Boarding & Day 13-18
No of pupils: B400 G260
Fees: (September 94) FB £12720 DAY £8481

CLAYESMORE PREPARATORY SCHOOL
Iwerne Minster, Blandford Forum, Dorset DT11 8PH
Tel: (01747) 811707
Head: H D Watson
Type: Co-educational Boarding & Day 3-13
No of pupils: B110 G90 No of Boarders F60 W10
Fees: (September 94) F/WB £8190 DAY £2775 - £5820

CLAYESMORE SCHOOL
Iwerne Minster, Blandford Forum, Dorset DT11 8LL
Tel: (01747) 812122
Head: D J Beeby
Type: Co-educational Boarding & Day 13-18
No of pupils: B170 G130 No of Boarders F240
Fees: (September 94) FB £10860 DAY £7605

CROFT HOUSE SCHOOL
Shillingstone, Blandford Forum, Dorset DT11 0QS
Tel: (01258) 860295
Head: M Hawkins
Type: Girls Boarding & Day 11-18
No of pupils: 130 No of Boarders F77 W29
Fees: (September 94) F/WB £9360 DAY £6600

HANFORD SCHOOL
Childe Okeford, Blandford Forum, Dorset DT11 8HL
Tel: (01258) 860219
Heads: Miss S Canning & Mr and M E Sharp
Type: Girls Boarding 7-13
No of pupils: 150 No of Boarders F150
Fees: (September 94) FB £7650

KNIGHTON HOUSE
Durweston, Blandford Forum, Dorset DT11 0PY
Tel: (01258) 452065
Head: R P Weatherly
Type: Co-educational Boarding & Day B4-7 G4-13
No of pupils: B20 G160 No of Boarders F110
Fees: (September 94) FB £8355 DAY £2280 - £6135

MILTON ABBEY SCHOOL
Blandford Forum, Dorset DT11 0BZ
Tel: (01258) 880484
Head: R H Hardy
Type: Boys Boarding & Day 13-18
No of pupils: 230 No of Boarders F224
Fees: (September 94) FB £11055 DAY £7380

Bournemouth

HOMEFIELD SCHOOL (PREPARATORY)
Iford Lane, Southbourne, Bournemouth, Dorset BH6 5NQ
Tel: (01202) 429483
Head: A C Partridge
Type: Co-educational Boarding & Day 3-12
No of pupils: B175 G75
Fees: (September 94) FB £8925 DAY £2385 - £3255

THE PARK SCHOOL
45 Queen's Park, South Drive, Bournemouth,
Dorset BH8 9BJ
Tel: (01202) 396640
Head: M Smyth
Type: Co-educational Day 4-12
No of pupils: 225
Fees: (September 94) £1986 - £2820

ST MARTIN'S SCHOOL
15 Stokewood Road, Bournemouth, Dorset BH3 7NA
Tel: (01202) 554483
Head: T Shenton
Type: Co-educational Day 4-12
No of pupils: B50 G57
Fees: (September 94) £1560 - £2025

ST THOMAS GARNET'S SCHOOL
Parkwood Road, Boscombe, Bournemouth, Dorset BH5 2DE
Tel: (01202) 420172
Head: P R Gillings
Type: Co-educational Day 2-11
No of pupils: B80 G70
Fees: (September 94) £2535

TALBOT HEATH
Rothesay Road, Bournemouth, Dorset BH4 9NJ
Tel: (01202) 761881
Head: Mrs C Dipple
Type: Girls Day & Boarding 3-18
No of pupils: 519 No of Boarders F28 W8
Fees: (September 94) FB £7266 - 8499 WB £7044 - £8277
DAY £1506 - £4944

TALBOT HOUSE PREPARATORY SCHOOL
8 Firs Glen Road, Bournemouth, Dorset BH9 2LR
Tel: (01202) 510348
Head: Mrs E H Stevenson
Type: Co-educational Day 4-12
No of pupils: B69 G74
Fees: (September 94) £1668 - £1823

WENTWORTH MILTON MOUNT
College Road, Bournemouth, Dorset BH5 2DY
Tel: (01202) 423266
Head: Miss S Coe
Type: Girls Boarding & Day 11-18
No of pupils: 265 No of Boarders F70 W30
Fees: (September 94) F/WB £8385 DAY £5241

Bridport

ST RONAN'S
Asker Mead, Bridport, Dorset DT6 4DA
Tel: (01308) 422128
Head: Mrs J A Fairbrother
Type: Co-educational Day 3-11
No of pupils: 60
Fees: (September 94) £1650

Christchurch

HOMEFIELD SCHOOL
Salisbury Road, Winkton, Christchurch, Dorset BH23 7AR
Tel: (01202) 476644
Head: A C Partridge
Type: Co-educational Boarding & Day 11-16
No of pupils: B250 G100
Fees: (September 94) FB £8925 DAY £2385 - £3705

Dorchester

DORCHESTER PREPARATORY SCHOOL
25/26 Icen Way, Dorchester, Dorset DT1 1EP
Tel: (01305) 264925
Head: J Rose
Type: Co-educational Day 3-13
No of pupils: B120 G80
Fees: (September 94) £1050 - £2670

ST GENEVIEVE'S SCHOOL
South Court, South Walk, Dorchester, Dorset DT1 1EB
Tel: (01305) 264898
Head: Mother Superior Sr Eugene
Type: Girls Day & Boarding 4-16 (Boys 4-11)
No of pupils: 200 No of Boarders W15
Fees: (September 93) WB £3000 DAY £1800 - £2100

SUNNINGHILL PREPARATORY SCHOOL
Herringston Road, Dorchester, Dorset DT1 2BS
Tel: (01305) 262306
Head: C Pring
Type: Co-educational Day 3-13
No of pupils: B78 G93
Fees: (September 94) £1200 - £2670

Lyme Regis

ALLHALLOWS SCHOOL
Rousdon, Lyme Regis, Dorset DT7 3RA
Tel: (01297) 626100
Head: P S Larkman
Type: Co-educational Boarding & Day 11-18
No of pupils: B159 G81 No of Boarders F180
Fees: (September 94) FB £10956 WB £10626
DAY £3864 - £5478

Poole

BUCKHOLME TOWERS
18 Commercial Road, Parkstone, Poole, Dorset BH14 0JW
Tel: (01202) 742871
Head: Mrs D J Stacey
Type: Co-educational Day 3-12
No of pupils: B79 G79
Fees: (September 94) £915 - £2235

ST JOSEPH'S CONVENT NURSERY SCHOOL
37 Parkstone Road, Poole, Dorset BH15 2NU
Tel: (01202) 674515
Head: Sr Germaine
Type: Co-educational Day 3-5
No of pupils: 40
Fees: On application

ST MONICA'S SCHOOL
The Yarrells, Upton, Poole, Dorset BH16 5EU
Tel: (01202) 622229
Head: Mrs Covell
Type: Co-educational Day 3-12
No of pupils: B27 G148
Fees: (September 94) £1290 - £4245

UPLANDS SCHOOL
40 St Osmund's Road, Parkstone, Poole, Dorset BH14 9JY
Tel: (01202) 742626
Head: Mrs L Dummett
Type: Co-educational Day 3-16
No of pupils: B185 G160
Fees: (September 94) £1455 - £3450

Shaftesbury

MOTCOMBE GRANGE SCHOOL
The Street, Motcombe, Shaftesbury, Dorset SP7 9HJ
Tel: (01747) 52426
Head: Mrs M R Williams
Type: Co-educational Day 3-11
No of pupils: B50 G50
Fees: (January 94) £2325

PORT REGIS
Motcombe Park, Shaftesbury, Dorset SP7 9QA
Tel: (01747) 852566
Head: P A Dix
Type: Co-educational Boarding & Day 4-13
No of pupils: B201 G107 No of Boarders F214 W30
Fees: (September 94) F/WB £10065 DAY £7350

ST MARY'S SCHOOL
Shaftesbury, Dorset SP7 9LP
Tel: (01747) 854005
Head: Sr M Campion Livesey
Type: Girls Boarding & Day 9-18
No of pupils: 300 No of Boarders F215
Fees: (September 94) FB £8750 - £9300 DAY £5640 - £5940

Sherborne

NEWELL HOUSE SCHOOL
Cornhill, Sherborne, Dorset DT9 3PL
Tel: (01935) 812584
Head: P J Dale
Type: Co-educational Day 3-12
No of pupils: B35 G25
Fees: (September 93) £1875 - £2550

★ **ST ANTONY'S-LEWESTON SCHOOL**
Sherborne, Dorset DT9 6EN
Tel: (01963) 210691
Head: Miss C Denley Lloyd
Type: Girls Boarding & Day 11-18
No of pupils: 285 No of Boarders F180
Fees: (September 94) FB £9831 DAY £6411

★ **ST ANTONY'S-LEWESTON PREPARATORY SCHOOL**
Sherborne, Dorset DT9 6EN
Tel: (01963) 210790
Head: Mrs S M Cook
Type: Co-educational Boarding & Day 3-11
No of pupils: 90
Fees: (May 95) B £6360 DAY £2790 - £3630

★ **SHERBORNE PREPARATORY SCHOOL**
Acreman Street, Sherborne, Dorset DT9 3NY
Tel: (01935) 812097
Head: R T M Lindsay
Type: Co-educational Day & Boarding $2^1/_2$ -13
No of pupils: B137 G65 No of Boarders F44 W16
Fees: (September 94) F/WB £7479 DAY £1215 - £4986

SHERBORNE SCHOOL
The Green, Sherborne, Dorset DT9 3AP
Tel: (01935) 812249
Head: P H Lapping
Type: Boys Boarding 13-18
No of pupils: 655 No of Boarders F630
Fees: (September 94) FB £12135 DAY £9255

★ **SHERBORNE SCHOOL FOR GIRLS**
Sherborne, Dorset DT9 3QN
Tel: (01935) 812245
Head: Miss J M Taylor
Type: Girls Boarding & Day 12-18
No of pupils: 453 No of Boarders F451
Fees: (September 94) FB £10800 DAY £7200

Swanage

THE OLD MALTHOUSE
Langton Matravers, Swanage, Dorset BH19 3HB
Tel: (01929) 422302
Head: J H Phillips
Type: Boys Boarding & Day 4-13 (Girls 4-7)
No of pupils: B114 G8 No of Boarders F66 W8
Fees: (September 94) F/WB £8355 DAY £2400 - £6336

Weymouth

★ **THORNLOW JUNIOR SCHOOL**
Connaught Road, Weymouth, Dorset DT4 0SA
Tel: (01305) 785703
Head: Mrs J D Crocker
Type: Co-educational Day & Boarding 4-11
No of pupils: B42 G18 No of Boarders F5 W12
Fees: (September 94) B from £6540 DAY from £2115

★ **THORNLOW SENIOR SCHOOL**
101 Buxton Road, Weymouth, Dorset DT4 9PR
Tel: (01305) 782977
Head: D H Crocker
Type: Co-educational Boarding & Day 11-16
No of pupils: B78 G24 No of Boarders F39 W24
Fees: (September 94) FB £7635 DAY £3480

Wimborne

CANFORD SCHOOL
Wimborne, Dorset BH21 3AD
Tel: (01202) 841254
Head: J D Lever
Type: Boys Boarding & Day 13-18 (Co-ed VIth form)
No of pupils: B430 G50 No of Boarders F362
Fees: (September 94) FB £11900 DAY £8925

CASTLE COURT PREPARATORY SCHOOL
The Knoll House, Knoll Lane, Corfe Mullen, Wimborne,
Dorset BH21 3RF
Tel: (01202) 694438
Head: R E Nicholl
Type: Co-educational Day 3-13
No of pupils: B148 G102
Fees: (September 94) £3150 - £6270

DUMPTON SCHOOL
Deans Grove House, Wimborne, Dorset BH21 7AF
Tel: (01202) 883818
Head: A G Watson
Type: Boys Day & Boarding 3-13
No of pupils: 220 No of Boarders F70
Fees: (September 94) F/WB £7425 DAY £1125 - £5730

Somerset

Bridgwater

QUANTOCK SCHOOL
Over Stowey, Bridgwater, Somerset TA5 1HD
Tel: (01278) 732252
Head: D T Peaster
Type: Co-educational Day & Boarding 8-16
No of pupils: B120 G60
Fees: (September 94) FB £6000 - £7800 WB £5700 - £7500
DAY £2100 - £3600

Bruton

BRUTON SCHOOL FOR GIRLS
Sunny Hill, Bruton, Somerset BA10 ONT
Tel: (01749) 812277
Head: Mrs J M Wade
Type: Girls Day & Boarding 8-18
No of pupils: 560 No of Boarders F190 W72
Fees: (September 94) F/WB £5943 - £6540 DAY £2946 - £3543

KING'S SCHOOL
Bruton, Somerset BA10 OED
Tel: (01749) 813326
Head: R I Smyth
Type: Boys Boarding & Day 13-18 (Co-ed VIth form)
No of pupils: B290 G16 No of Boarders F251
Fees: (September 94) FB £10650 DAY £7545

Burnham-on-Sea

ST CHRISTOPHER'S
93 Berrow Road, Burnham-on-Sea, Somerset TA8 2NY
Tel: (01278) 782234
Head: Mrs S P Morrell-Davies
Type: Girls Day & Boarding 3-13 (Boys 3-11)
No of pupils: 124 No of Boarders F24
Fees: (September 94) F/WB £7350 DAY £2250 - £4410

Chard

CHARD INDEPENDENT SCHOOL
Fore Street, Chard, Somerset TA20 1QE
Tel: (01460) 63234
Head: C Organ
Type: Co-educational Day 3-11
No of pupils: B65 G46
Fees: (September 94) £1980 - £2070

Crewkerne

★ **PERROTT HILL SCHOOL**
North Perrott, Crewkerne, Somerset TA18 7SL
Tel: (01460) 72051
Head: J E A Barnes
Type: Co-educational Boarding & Day 3-13
No of pupils: B103 G26 No of Boarders F16 W18
Fees: (September 94) F/WB £7320 DAY £1575 - £5265

ST MARTIN'S INDEPENDENT SCHOOL
24 Abbey Street, Crewkerne, Somerset TA18 7HY
Tel: (01460) 73265
Head: Mrs J A Murrell
Type: Co-educational Day 4-13
No of pupils: B50 G50
Fees: (September 94) £1200 - £2850

Glastonbury

ABBEY SCHOOL
Magdalene Street, Glastonbury, Somerset BA6 9EJ
Tel: (01458) 832902
Head: Mrs K L Cookson
Type: Co-educational Day 3-8
No of pupils: B87 G63
Fees: (September 94) £2325 - £2475

★ **EDGARLEY HALL**
Glastonbury, Somerset BA6 8LD
Tel: (01458) 832446
Head: R J Smyth
Type: Co-educational Boarding & Day 8-13
No of pupils: B262 G178 No of Boarders F266
Fees: (September 94) FB £9450 DAY £6180

Highbridge

ROSSHOLME SCHOOL
East Brent, Highbridge, Somerset TA9 4JA
Tel: (01278) 760219
Head: Mrs S J Webb
Type: Girls Boarding & Day 7-16 (Co-ed 3-7)
No of pupils: B6 G78 No of Boarders F20
Fees: (September 94) FB £6495 - £6990 WB £6375 - £6870
DAY £1590 - £3570

Shepton Mallet

ALL HALLOWS
Cranmore Hall, East Cranmore, Shepton Mallet,
Somerset BA4 4SF
Tel: (01749) 880227
Head: P F Ketterer
Type: Co-educational Boarding & Day 3-14
No of pupils: B132 G87 No of Boarders F80 W17
Fees: (September 94) F/WB £7956 DAY £2595 - £5190

Street

MILLFIELD SCHOOL
Street, Somerset BA16 OYD
Tel: (01458) 42291
Head: C S Martin
Type: Co-educational Boarding & Day 13-18
No of pupils: B754 G464 No of Boarders F923
Fees: (September 94) FB £12930 DAY £7920

Taunton

BEEHIVE SCHOOL
68 Wellington Road, Taunton, Somerset TA1 5AP
Tel: (01823) 333638
Head: J P Garrett
Type: Co-educational Day 4-11
No of pupils: B70 G70
Fees: (September 94) £1185 - £1200

KING'S COLLEGE
Taunton, Somerset TA1 3DX
Tel: (01823) 272708
Head: R S Funnell
Type: Co-educational Boarding & Day 13-18
No of pupils: B338 G109 No of Boarders F375
Fees: (September 94) FB £10980 DAY £7380

KING'S HALL SCHOOL
Pyrland, Kingston Road, Taunton, Somerset TA2 8AA
Tel: (01823) 272431
Head: Mrs M Willson
Type: Co-educational Boarding & Day 3-13
No of pupils: B243 G167 No of Boarders F45 W35
Fees: (September 94) FB £4560 - £7650 WB £4290 - £7380
DAY £1650 - £5400

QUEEN'S COLLEGE
Trull Road, Taunton, Somerset TA1 4QS
Tel: (01823) 272559
Head: C Bradnock
Type: Co-educational Boarding & Day 8-18
No of pupils: B348 G274 No of Boarders F231
Fees: (September 94) FB £8820 DAY £5760

QUEEN'S COLLEGE JUNIOR SCHOOL
Trull Road, Taunton, Somerset TA1 4QR
Tel: (01823) 272990
Head: P N Lee-Smith
Type: Co-educational Day & Boarding 8-12
No of pupils: B85 G85 No of Boarders F50
Fees: (September 94) FB £4080 - £7425
DAY £2640 - £4920

TAUNTON PREPARATORY SCHOOL
Staplegrove Road, Taunton, Somerset TA2 6AE
Tel: (01823) 349250
Head: A D Wood
Type: Co-educational Day & Boarding 3-13
No of pupils: 410 No of Boarders F45
Fees: (September 94) FB £4290 - £8310 DAY £1320 - £5490

TAUNTON SCHOOL
Taunton, Somerset TA2 6AD
Tel: (01823) 349200/349223
Head: B B Sutton
Type: Co-educational Boarding & Day 12-18
No of pupils: B280 G238 No of Boarders F238
Fees: (September 94) FB £11070 DAY £7080

Watchet

BUCKLAND SCHOOL
7 St Decumans Road, Watchet, Somerset TA23 0HR
Tel: (01984) 631314
Type: Co-educational Day 2-9
No of pupils: 40
Fees: (September 94) £1344

Wellington

WELLINGTON SCHOOL
South Street, Wellington, Somerset TA21 8NT
Tel: (01823) 664511
Head: A J Rogers
Type: Co-educational Boarding & Day 10-19
No of pupils: B457 G381 No of Boarders F205
Fees: (September 94) FB £7698 DAY £4194

Wells

WELLS CATHEDRAL JUNIOR SCHOOL
10 New Street, Wells, Somerset BA5 2LQ
Tel: (01749) 672291
Head: P M Peabody
Type: Co-educational Boarding & Day 4-11
No of pupils: B100 G85 No of Boarders F26
Fees: (September 94) FB £7590 DAY £2436 - £4683

WELLS CATHEDRAL SCHOOL
Wells, Somerset BA5 2ST
Tel: (01749) 672117
Head: J S Baxter
Type: Co-educational Boarding & Day 4-18
No of pupils: B398 G398 No of Boarders F306
Fees: (September 94) FB £8688 DAY £5103

Winscombe

★ **SIDCOT SCHOOL**
Winscombe, North Somerset BS25 1PD
Tel: (01934) 843102
Head: C Greenfield
Type: Co-educational Boarding & Day 9-18
No of pupils: 390
Fees: (September 94) FB £9282 DAY from £4101

Yeovil

CHILTON CANTELO SCHOOL
Chilton Cantelo, Yeovil, Somerset BA22 8BG
Tel: (01935) 850555
Head: D S von Zeffman
Type: Co-educational Boarding & Day 8-18
No of pupils: B70 G60 No of Boarders F80
Fees: (September 94) FB £6225 - £8385 DAY £3090 - £4710

KING'S BRUTON PRE-PREPARATORY & JUNIOR SCHOOL
Hazlegrove House, Sparkford, Yeovil, Somerset BA22 7JA
Tel: (01963) 440314
Head: Rev B Bearcroft
Type: Boys Boarding & Day 3-13 (Girls 8-13)
No of pupils: 258 No of Boarders F120
Fees: (September 93) FB £7725 DAY £2655 - £5400

THE PARK SCHOOL
Yeovil, Somerset BA20 1DH
Tel: (01935) 23514
Head: P W Bate
Type: Co-educational Day & Boarding 3-16
No of pupils: B45 G132 No of Boarders F15 W3
Fees: (September 94) FB £6900 - £7800 WB £6300 - £7200
DAY £1575 - £4500

Wiltshire

Calne

ST MARY'S SCHOOL
Calne, Wiltshire SN11 ODF
Tel: (01249) 815899
Head: Miss D H Burns
Type: Girls Boarding & Day 11-18
No of pupils: 318 No of Boarders F285
Fees: (September 94) FB £10950 DAY £6495

Chippenham

GRITTLETON HOUSE SCHOOL
Grittleton, Chippenham, Wiltshire SN14 6AP
Tel: (01249) 782434
Head: P Moore
Type: Co-educational Day 3-16
No of pupils: B137 G80
Fees: (September 94) £1755 - £3375

THE INTERNATIONAL SCHOOL OF CHOUEIFAT
Ashwicke Hall, Marshfield, Chippenham, Wiltshire SN14 8AG
Tel: (01225) 891841
Head: R Bistany
Type: Co-educational Boarding 8-18
No of pupils: B174 G58 No of Boarders F141
Fees: (September 94) FB £8700 - £9500

Colerne

★ **CALDER HOUSE SCHOOL**
Colerne, Nr Bath, Wiltshire SN14 8BN
Tel: (01225) 742329
Head: Mrs S Agombar
Type: Co-educational Day 5-13
No of pupils: maximum 50
Fees: (May 95) £5100 - £5700

Corsham

HEYWOOD PREPARATORY SCHOOL
The Priory, Priory Street, Corsham, Wiltshire SN13 0AP
Tel: (01249) 713379
Heads: M Hall & P Hall
Type: Co-educational Day 3-11
No of pupils: B112 G92
Fees: (September 94) £1995 - £2385

Devizes

DAUNTSEY'S SCHOOL
West Lavington, Devizes, Wiltshire SN10 4HE
Tel: (01380) 812446
Head: C R Evans
Type: Co-educational Boarding & Day 11-18
No of pupils: B355 G280 No of Boarders F295
Fees: (September 94) FB £10149 DAY £6249

THE MILL SCHOOL
Potterne, Devizes, Wiltshire SN10 5TE
Tel: (01380) 723011
Head: J M Eman
Type: Co-educational Day 3-11
No of pupils: B30 G18
Fees: (September 94) £1350 - £3150

Marlborough

KINGSBURY HILL HOUSE
34 Kingsbury Street, Marlborough, Wiltshire SN8 1JA
Tel: (01672) 512680
Head: M Innes Williams
Type: Co-educational Day 3-13
No of pupils: 110
Fees: (September 94) £2340 - £4080

★ **MARLBOROUGH COLLEGE**
Marlborough, Wiltshire SN8 1PA
Tel: (01672) 515511
Head: E J H Gould
Type: Co-educational Boarding 13-18
No of pupils: B525 G271 No of Boarders F769
Fees: (September 94) FB £12120 DAY £8550

ST ANDREW SCHOOL
Ogbourne St Andrew, Marlborough, Wiltshire
Tel: (01672) 841291
Head: Miss S Platt
Type: Co-educational Day 3-11
No of pupils: B18 G23
Fees: (September 94) £1920 - £3135

Melksham

STONAR SCHOOL
Melksham, Wiltshire SN12 8NT
Tel: (01225) 702309
Head: Mrs S Hopkinson
Type: Girls Boarding & Day 4-18
No of pupils: 520 No of Boarders F280 W26
Fees: (September 94) F/WB £8406 - £9180 DAY £2250 - £5085

Salisbury

CHAFYN GROVE SCHOOL
Bourne Avenue, Salisbury, Wiltshire SP1 1LR
Tel: (01722) 333423
Head: D P Duff-Mitchell
Type: Co-educational Boarding & Day 4-13
No of pupils: B153 G78 No of Boarders F20 W50
Fees: (September 94) F/WB £7290 DAY £2550 - £5445

FLAMBEAUX MONTESSORI SCHOOL/DAY NURSERY
18 Burford Road, Salisbury, Wiltshire SP2 8AN
Tel: (01722) 322179
Head: Mrs N M Brinn
Type: Co-educational Day 1-7
No of pupils: 100
Fees: (September 94) £141 - £720

THE GODOLPHIN SCHOOL
Milford Hill, Salisbury, Wiltshire SP1 2RA
Tel: (01722) 333059
Head: Mrs H A Fender
Type: Girls Boarding & Day 7-18 (Boarding from 11)
No of pupils: 400 No of Boarders F210
Fees: (September 94) F/WB £10266 DAY £6150

LA RETRAITE LEEHURST SCHOOL
Campbell Road, Salisbury, Wiltshire SP1 3BQ
Tel: (01722) 333094
Head: Mrs R Simmons
Type: Girls Day 3-18 (Boys 3-7)
No of pupils: B12 G190
Fees: (September 94) £2460 - £4260

★ **LEADEN HALL**
70 The Close, Salisbury, Wiltshire SP1 2EP
Tel: (01722) 334700
Head: Mrs D Watkins
Type: Girls Day & Boarding 3-12+
No of pupils: 184 No of Boarders F20
Fees: (September 94) B £6240 DAY £2220 - £3480

NORTHAW SCHOOL
West Tytherley, Salisbury, Wiltshire SP5 1NH
Tel: (01980) 862345
Head: P E Thwaites
Type: Co-educational Boarding & Day 4-13
No of pupils: B99 G57 No of Boarders F42 W30
Fees: (September 94) F/WB £7830 DAY £2760 - £5820

★ **SALISBURY CATHEDRAL SCHOOL**
1 The Close, Salisbury, Wiltshire SP1 2EQ
Tel: (01722) 322652
Head: C J A Helyer
Type: Co-educational Day & Boarding $3\frac{1}{2}$ -13
No of pupils: B195 G107 No of Boarders F73
Fees: (September 94) FB £7440 DAY £2910 - £5610

★ **SANDROYD**
Tollard Royal, Salisbury, Wiltshire SP5 5QD
Tel: (01725) 516264
Head: M J Hatch
Type: Boys Boarding 7-13
No of pupils: 137
Fees: (September 94) DAY £7200

SWAN SCHOOL FOR BOYS
26 Elm Grove Road, Salisbury, Wiltshire
Tel: (01722) 334522
Head: Mrs B L Healy
Type: Boys Day 3-11
No of pupils: 130
Fees: (September 94) £2100

Swindon

★ **PINEWOOD SCHOOL**
Bourton, Swindon, Wiltshire SN6 8HZ
Tel: (01793) 782205
Head: H G C Boddington
Type: Co-educational Boarding & Day 4-13
No of pupils: B121 G59 No of Boarders F51
Fees: (September 94) FB £7560 DAY £2550 - £5760

PRIOR PARK PREPARATORY SCHOOL
Cricklade, Swindon, Wiltshire SN6 6BB
Tel: (01793) 750275
Head: G B Hobern
Type: Co-educational Boarding & Day 7-13
No of pupils: B136 G75 No of Boarders F132
Fees: (September 93) F/WB £6426 DAY £4488

Warminster

STOURBRIDGE HOUSE SCHOOL
Castle Street, Mere, Warminster, Wiltshire BA12 6JQ
Tel: (01747) 860165
Head: Mrs E Coward
Type: Co-educational Day 3-8
No of pupils: B30 G30
Fees: (September 94) £2208 - £2328

WARMINSTER SCHOOL
Church Street, Warminster, Wiltshire BA12 8PJ
Tel: (01985) 213038
Head: T D Holgate
Type: Co-educational Boarding & Day 4-18
No of pupils: B265 G220 No of Boarders F300
Fees: (September 94) FB £7950 - £8700 DAY £1560 - £5085

Display Listings of
Schools in the South West

Avon

Badminton School
AVO

Badminton School

Westbury-on-Trym,
Bristol, Avon BS9 3BA
Tel: 0117 9623141 Fax: 0117 962 8963

Headmaster: Mr C J T Gould, MA, PGCE, FRSA
Type: Girls' Boarding & Day School
Age range: 5-11 (Juniors); 11-18 (Seniors)
No. of pupils enrolled as at 1.5.95: 360
Fees per annum:
Day: £2850-£5925; Boarding: £7995-£10,725

Religious affiliation: Non-denominational

Most girls get 9 or 10 GCSEs and 3 A levels.
90% of the Sixth Form go on to degree
courses, including Oxford and Cambridge.

The School encourages a mature and friendly
atmosphere and has a strong tradition in
Music and Science. Excellence and all-round
ability are equally valued.

Entry and Scholarship Examinations:
These take place in late January each year,
with awards of up to half fees for girls aged
11, 12 and 13, or entering the Sixth Form,
and special Music Scholarships at any age.

Badminton School is a charitable institution
for the purpose of educating children.

Bristol Grammar School

EX SPINIS UVAS

1532

(Founded 1532)

University Road, Bristol, Avon BS8 1SR
Tel: (Upper School) 01179 736006;
(Lower School) 01179 736109
Fax: 01179 467485

Head of Upper School: Charles E Martin, MA
Head of Lower School: Mrs Jane Jenkins, BA
Type: Independent Co-educational Day School
Age range: 7-18
No. of pupils enrolled as at 1.2.95: Total 1221
Junior: 142 Boys 62 Girls
Senior (including Sixth Form): 680 Boys 337 Girls
Sixth Form: 188 Boys 90 Girls
Fees per annum:
Upper School: £3705; Lower School: £2205

Religious affiliation: Interdenominational
Member of: Upper School: HMC, GBA;
Lower School: IAPS

The Lower School admits pupils aged 7-11;
the Upper School admits pupils 11-18.

Curriculum: The Lower School curriculum
includes Religious Education, English,
Mathematics, History, Geography, Science,
Art, Technology, IT, Music, French and
Physical Education. Art, Drama and Music
are particularly encouraged.

The Upper School provides the National
Curriculum +. Setting is used in some subjects.
There is no streaming. In the first two years
all pupils follow a curriculum, which includes
English, Mathematics, Science, French, History,
Geography, Technology, IT, Latin, Religious
Studies, Art, Music and Physical Education.
Further up the School other subjects become

available such as Russian, German, Greek and
Economics, and at the end of the Fifth Year all
pupils take some 10 GCSEs drawn from the core
subjects of English, Mathematics, Science and
French, together with a selection of their subjects
chosen from a carefully balanced range of
options. The Sixth Form provides a flexible
range of options chosen from English, Mathematics, the Sciences, Modern Languages, Classics,
History, Geography, Economics, Business
Studies, Computer Studies, Art and Music.
In addition, all pupils follow General Studies
courses and attend a diverse programme of weekly
lectures by distinguished visiting speakers.
After A levels pupils proceed to Universities
and Higher Education around the country.

Academic and leisure facilities: Although
organised separately, both parts of the School
occupy the same impressive site adjacent to
the University. They share many of the same
facilities and opportunities for every kind
of sporting, cultural and extra-curricular
activity abound. During the past decade
new class-rooms have been built and
the laboratories have been completely
refurbished. A music school was opened in
1987, as were a theatre and language centre
in 1990, a sports hall in 1991, an art school
in 1992, and a magnificent technology centre
in 1994. A short bus ride away from the main
site are over 50 acres of playing fields,
including an all-weather hockey pitch.

In both parts of the School pupils participate
in a weekly programme of games and activities
and, in the Upper School, the Duke of Edinburgh
Award Scheme is a popular option. Regular
excursions are made abroad and there is
a well established programme of European
and Russian school-to-school exchanges.

Admission procedures: Enquiries about
admission procedures and scholarships should
be made to the appropriate part of the School.
Parents of prospective entrants are welcome
to visit the School at any time by appointment.

Bristol Grammar School is a charity which
exists for the provision and conduct in or
near the City of Bristol of a day school for
boys and girls.

CLIFTON HIGH SCHOOL

(Founded 1877)

College Road,
Clifton, Bristol,
Avon BS8 3JD
Tel: 0117 973 0201 Fax: 0117 923 8962

Headmistress: Mrs J D Walters, MA
Type: Independent Day and Boarding School
Age range: 3-18. Boarders from 16
No. of pupils enrolled as at 1.1.95: 750
Junior, Preparatory and Nursery (3-11): 73 Boys 232 Girls
Senior: 445 Girls (including 115 in Sixth Form)
Fees per annum:
Day: £780-£4575; Weekly Boarding: £8220;
Full Boarding: £8655

Religious affiliation: Non-denominational

Member of: GSA, SHA

Curriculum: The curriculum is broad and balanced – English, History, Geography, Religious Studies, French, Spanish, German, Latin, Greek, Classical Civilisation, Mathematics, Physics, Chemistry, Biology, Information Technology, Technology, Home Economics, Textiles, Art, Music, Economics, Government & Politics, Theatre Studies, Physical Education and Games. Girls normally take nine or ten GCSE subjects and three or four A Levels. 95% of the Sixth Form go on to degree courses, including Oxford and Cambridge. There is a wide range of sports and extra curricular activities, including the Duke of Edinburgh Award Scheme.

Academic and leisure facilities: The School occupies an attractive position in the centre of Clifton. There has been a continuous programme of development over the last five years: a new Sixth Form Centre, Senior and Middle School Libraries, Computer Centre, Creative Arts complex, Electronics and Technology Laboratories, Lecture Theatre. There is also on site a large indoor heated Swimming Pool, a Music School and Assembly Hall with stage. The Junior and Preparatory Departments share a number of these facilities.

Pastoral Care: All girls from the age of 11 years have their own personal tutor. Through the tutorial system each pupil's progress and well-being is carefully monitored for the whole of her school career.

Entry requirements: Pupils applying for entry from the age of seven years are expected to take the School's own Entrance Examination. Children under seven years are interviewed for entry. For the Sixth Form a minimum of five GCSE grades at A and B are required.

Clifton High School is a registered charity and aims to provide a first-class education for girls up to the age of 18 years and for boys to the age of 11 years.

The Hall School (Pre-preparatory for Sidcot School)

(Founded 1966)

Winscombe,
Avon BS25 1PD
Tel: 01934 844118 Fax: 01934 844181

Head: Wendy Wardman, CertEd
Type: Pre-preparatory School
Age range: 3-8
No of pupils enrolled as at 1.1.95: 56
32 Boys 24 Girls
Fees per annum: £1425-£2790

Religious affiliation: Quaker

Member of: ISJC (via Sidcot School)

Curriculum: The School follows the National Curriculum with emphasis on the basic skills. Computers are used throughout school, and Sidcot School's specialist sport and other facilities are used. After school clubs include swimming and French. Dyslexic specialists visit the school. Horse riding is also offered.

Entry requirements: By interview.

The aim of the Sidcot School Charitable Trust is the education of children in a Quaker and caring environment.

Redland High School for Girls

(Founded 1882)

Redland Court,
Redland,
Bristol,
Avon BS6 7EF
Tel: 0117 9245796

Headmistress: Mrs Carol Lear, BA(Hons)
Type: Independent Girls' Day School
Age range: 4-18
No of pupils enrolled as at 1.5.95: 640
Junior: 165 Girls; Senior: 475 Girls
Sixth Form: 124 Girls
Fees per annum: £2451-£3777

Religious affiliation: Non-denominational

Member of: GSA, SHA

Curriculum: Art, Biology, Business Studies, Chemistry, Classical Civilisation, Computer Studies, CDT, Economics, English, French, Geography, German, Greek, History, History of Art, Home Economics, Latin, Mathematics, Music, Physics, Physical Education, Religious Education, Social and Environmental Biology, Spanish.

Entry requirements: Entrance examination, 11+ January. Entrance tests - Juniors - January.

The School is a friendly, caring and purposeful community with high academic achievement. Girls are encouraged to realise their potential and develop their talents. We provide a full and balanced education which will help them to form happy relationships, equip them for a career and creative leisure, and enable them to feel of value and capable of assuming responsibility.

The Redland High School for Girls is a Charitable Trust which has a good academic record, and provides a broad and balanced education to develop the ability and potential of each individual.

Institutions offering Further Education appear in their own Section

---

Specialists in consultancy, design, production and publication of:

- ✂ Prospectuses
- ✂ Videos
- ✂ Exhibitions
- ✂ Marketing
- ✂ Newsletters
- ✂ Magazines
- ✂ School Histories
- ✂ Research

Our experience and quality of craftsmanship enable us to offer a service which we believe is unequalled by any other organisation.

For a prompt quotation with no obligation please telephone, fax or write to:

John Catt Educational Ltd

Great Glemham,
Saxmundham, Suffolk IP17 2DH

Tel: 01728 663666   *Fax: 01728 663415*

AVO

The Royal School

(Founded 1864)

*Lansdown Road,
Bath BA1 5SZ
Tel: 01225 313877 Fax: 01225 420338*

Head: Mrs Emma McKendrick, BA, GSA, SHA
Type: Independent School
Age range: 3-18 Boarders from 7-18
No of pupils enrolled as at 8.2.95: 332
Junior: 12 Boys 84 Girls
Senior: 157 Girls; Sixth Form: 79 Girls
Fees per term:
Day: £927-£1962; Boarding: £2997-£3560
Sixth Form Day: £1962; Boarding: £3560
(Sessional Nursery Fees)

Religious affiliation: Church of England

Member of: GBGSA

Curriculum: Through a broad and balanced curriculum and a varied programme of activities we aim to prepare individual students for a happy and purposeful future. All students follow the National Curriculum up to 16, and a wide range of A and AS levels is offered in the Sixth Form. Strong music, drama and PE departments enter students for specialist examinations and competitions. Over 90% of students go on to Higher Education.

Entry requirements: Entrance is through assessment of a candidate's work and where possible, interviews. The School welcomes candidates working towards Common Entrance. Scholarships can be taken at 11+, 13+ and 16+.

Examinations offered: GCSE (LEAG/MEG/MES/SEG/NEA) depending on the subject. A/AS levels (Cambridge/London/Oxford and Cambridge/AEB/JMB according to subject). LAMDA, Associated Board.

Academic and leisure facilities: Our separate Pre-prep and Junior Departments, Main School and purpose built Sixth Form Centre are all housed on our 16 acre site on the outskirts of Bath. Students relax in comfortable and modern boarding accommodation. Up-to-date classroom facilities include recently developed technology workshops. The open-air swimming pool and 20 acres of playing fields are enjoyed both during and outside the school day.

Royal School exists to provide for such charitable works as advance education and in particular boarding education for girls.

Devon

Mount St Mary's Convent School

(Founded 1896)

*Wonford Road,
Exeter, Devon EX2 4PF
Tel: 01392 436770 Fax: 01392 423572*

Head: Sister Eileen Delaney
Type: Girls Day School
Age range: 3-18
No of pupils enrolled as at 1.5.95: 450
Fees per term: £800-£1095

Religious affiliation: Roman Catholic

Member of: GSA

- Excellent facilities

- Excellent standards in public examinations, GCSE, A levels and GNVQ

- Small classes

- Individual attention

- Good discipline

- Strong links with home

Entry requirements: Interview and test appropriate to the child's age.

Mount St Mary's Convent School, which is a registered charity, exists to provide an excellent education for local children.

A list of useful Educational Associations appears at the back of this book

Sands School

(Founded 1987)

Greylands,
48 East Street,
Ashburton,
Devon TQ13 7AX
Tel: 01364 653666

Head: Mr Sean Bellamy, MA(Cantab), PGCE
Type: Democratic Day School
Age range: 10-18
No of pupils enrolled as at 1.5.95: 40
Junior: 9 Boys 6 Girls
Senior: 14 Boys 10 Girls
Sixth Form: 4 Boys
Fees per annum: £2970-£3045
Bursaries available in cases of need

Religious affiliation: None

Member of: International Federation of Democratic Schools

Sands School is the South West's only democratic school. It was designed by students and staff together. Its principles include respect for the individual, democratic decision making and a wide curriculum based on what children choose to learn as well as what they expect to learn. It offers an exciting and supportive atmosphere that young people find both relevant and rewarding. Although Sands puts the wellbeing of the child above academic success, the National League Tables show our exam results to be better than all South Devon's comprehensive schools.

Sands School, which is a registered charity, exists to provide quality education and give young people opportunity to co-ordinate and develop an ideal curriculum according to their individual needs.

DEV

St Bernard's School

(Founded over 50 years)

*9 Courtenay Road, Newton Abbot,
South Devon TQ12 1HP
Tel: 01626 65424 Fax: 01626 336489*

Head: R Dudley-Cooke
Type: Preparatory Day School and Nursery
Age range: 2-11
No of pupils enrolled as at 1.5.95: 100; 35 Boys 65 Girls
Fees per annum: £720-£2574

Religious affiliation: Non-denominational

Member of: ISAI

"A CARING ENVIRONMENT FOR THE FULL REALISATION OF A PUPIL'S POTENTIAL"

The School is a Preparatory Day School for girls and boys 3+-11. There is also a Nursery for the under 3. It offers a family environment with high academic standards and very high success rate to both Grammar Schools and Independent Schools of parental choice.

A feature and policy of St Bernard's is the low pupil-teacher ratio. The largest class has less than 15 pupils.

All pupils are actively involved in sporting activities. Pupils are encouraged to participate in extra curriculum activities.

Full details on application.

St Michael's School

(Founded 1832)

Tawstock Court,
Tawstock,
Barnstaple,
North Devon EX31 3HY
Tel: 01271 43242 Fax: 01271 46771

Head: Mr R K Yetzes, BEd(Hons), CertEd
Type: Co-educational Preparatory School
with a Pre-Preparatory Department
Age range: 3-13+. Boarders from 6
No. of pupils enrolled as at 1.5.95:
131 Boys   76 Girls
Fees per annum:
Day: £2340-£4695; Boarding: £5250-£7620

Religious denomination: Church of England

Member of: IAPS, ISIS, BSA

Academic: The National Curriculum is covered but with substantial extra areas covered such as languages, where all children study French and German from the age of 7 and Spanish is an option. First Aid, Self-Defence and Food Studies are integrated alongside Technology, Design and Computing.

Sports: There is an extensive games and physical education programme with all major games being played, in addition to minor sports such as badminton, cross-country, Budo, basketball, squash and archery.

Activities: Children may pursue a large number of activites including horse-riding, quad bike riding, pottery, carpentry, chess, drama, computing, trampolining, short tennis, Brownies, and Outward Bound activities.

Music and the Arts: A full-time Director of Music oversees an energetic programme of group, ensemble and class music. The School's choir has performed on radio and television, its record in raising money has led to them gaining a place in The Child of Achievement Awards. Approximately two-thirds of the school receives individual instrument or singing lessons.

Surroundings and campus: Set in the beautiful North Devon countryside, St Michael's has over 30 acres looking across the Taw Valley. Woods and playing fields surround the magnificent main house and the facilities have been supplemented by a Sports Hall, Squash Courts, Swimming Pool, Computer, Language and Science Laboratories.

Boarding: Our pupils have excellent pastoral supervision and this is maintained into our

boarding area where Houseparents and Matrons work hard to provide the home away from home.

PUPILS HAVE GAINED OVER 20 SCHOLARSHIPS TO MAJOR PUBLIC SCHOOLS IN THE LAST THREE YEARS.

Entry is by interview and/or testing. Some scholarships and bursaries available.

The St Michael's School Charitable Trust exists to provide high quality education for boys and girls.

In addition to the Scholarship Announcements, which appear at the start of this section, there is up-to-date information on Assisted Places, Reserved Entrance Awards – and advice on finding the fees

DEV

Trinity School

Buckeridge Road,
Teignmouth,
Devon TQ14 8LY
Tel: 01626 774138

Headmaster: C J Ashby, BSc, PGCE
Type: Co-educational Boarding and Day School
Age range: 3-18. Boarders from 6
No. of pupils enrolled as at 1.1.95:
301 (including Nursery)
Junior: 68 Boys 65 Girls; Senior: 91 Boys 77 Girls
Fees per annum:
Day: £2460-£3930; Boarding: £7050-£7800

Location: Set in attractive parkland in an area of outstanding natural beauty overlooking Lyme Bay.

Religious affiliation: Anglican/Roman Catholic/Non-denominational intake

Member of: ISIS, ISAI, SHA, CCSS

Curriculum: The Senior Department prepares pupils to achieve excellent results at GCSE level. GCSE courses offered include most traditional subjects, but also Home Economics, Information Technology and Music. GNVQ Intermediate Business is also offered from 14-16 years. There are over thirty extra-curricular activities/games; career advice and a social education course is provided. From 11-14 years children study Home Economics, IT, Design Technology, Environmental Studies, Media Studies, Communication Skills and German, alongside traditional subjects. Post-16 education is tailored to the needs of the individual including the sharing of resources with other Schools and Colleges. The School offers vocational courses with A levels *eg* Business and Finance advanced GNVQ. The Preparatory Department maintains traditional standards while embracing the new developments in education. It follows a curriculum which includes Science, Information Technology, French and German, with a full sport, PE, clubs and hobbies programme.

Pastoral: A strong pastoral structure exists with personal tutors. Residential Staff : Boarders 1:8

Comfortable single or twin study bedrooms.

Entry requirements: Entrance test, interview and report from previous school.

Trinity School is a charitable institute for the education of children. The School aims to fulfil the potential of each child by focusing attention on each individual. Sporting, music and Academic Scholarships and Forces Bursaries are available.

Dorset

St Antony's-Leweston School

(Founded 1891)

Sherborne, Dorset DT9 6EN
Tel: 01963 210691 Fax: 01963 210786

Headmistress: Miss Christine Denley Lloyd,
BA(Hons), FIMgt, FRSA
Type: Catholic Independent Boarding
and Day School for Girls
Age range: 11-18. Boarders from 11
No of pupils enrolled as at 1.5.95: 285
Fees per annum: Day: £6411; Boarding: £9831

Religious affiliation: Roman Catholic foundation but all denominations welcomed.

Member of: GBGSA, GSA, BSA

With growing pressures for flexibility St Antony's-Leweston offers all the options of boarding, flexi-boarding and 'extended day' enabling girls to gain maximum benefit of boarding experience while still being able to maintain established social and family contact. Highly successful academically with some of the finest Science and Design and Technology facilities in the country. Thriving Sixth Form, high Science take up at A level.

Numerous prestigious awards and distinctions in Music and Drama. Range of modern languages. Combined Music, Art, Drama and social activities with Sherborne School and Milton Abbey. Specialist Dyslexia and EFL departments. Transport provision for day girls. Facilities include Sports Hall, Swimming Pool and Multi-Gym, Arts Studio and modern Health Centre. Academic and Music Scholarships available.

St Antony's-Leweston School is a charitable trust for the purpose of educating children. Registered Charity No. 295175.

St Antony's-Leweston Preparatory School

Sherborne, Dorset DT9 6EN
Tel: 01963 210790 Fax: 01963 210790

Headteacher: Mrs S M Cook, BA(Hons), PGCE
Type: Preparatory for Boys and Girls 3-11 (Day)
and Girls 7-11 (Boarding).
Separate Nursery and Pre-Prep
Age range: 3-11
No of pupils enrolled as at 1.5.95: 90
Fees per term: Boarding: £2120
Day: Upper Preparatory £1210
Lower Preparatory £1090
Pre-Preparatory £930
Nursery: £83 for each half day and
pro-rata up to £415 for 5 half days

Religious affiliation: Roman Catholic foundation but all denominations welcomed.

Established Christian Preparatory School combining traditional values and excellence in teaching with modern facilities and equipment. Purpose built with bright spacious classrooms and all amenities. Situated in 40 acres of beautiful Dorset parkland on same campus as Senior School. Friendly, relaxed atmosphere, high academic standards together with musical, artistic and sporting excellence. Well qualified staff, separate Nursery and Pre-Prep. After School clubs, supervised Prep; tea and boarding for girls from seven available on a flexible basis,

daily transport provision to surrounding towns and villages including Yeovil, Sherborne and Dorchester. Added advantage of many shared facilities with the senior school including Sports Hall, Swimming Pool, Tennis Courts, Hockey and Rugby Pitches, superb Design and Technology Centre and fully equipped science laboratories. French taught from five, preparation for Common Entrance.

St Antony's-Leweston Preparatory School is a charitable trust for the purpose of educating children. Registered Charity No. 295175.

DOR

Sherborne Preparatory School

(Founded 1885)

Acreman Street, Sherborne, Dorset DT9 3NY
Tel: 01935 812097 Fax: 01935 813948

Head: Mr R T M Lindsay, MA(Cantab), CertEd
Type: Independent Co-educational
Boarding and Day School
Age range: 2½-13½. Boarders from 7
No. of pupils enrolled as at 1.5.95: 202
Pre-Prep: 34 Boys 20 Girls
Prep: 103 Boys 45 Girls
Fees per term: Pre-Prep: Half-day £405; Full Day £945
Prep: Day £1662; Boarding: £2493

Religious affiliation: Church of England

Member of: IAPS

Curriculum: Boys and girls are prepared for the Common Entrance Examination and for scholarships to Independent Senior Schools.

Entry requirements: Interview if possible and report from previous school.

Situated in lovely grounds in the town of Sherborne, the School has a long tradition of academic, musical and sporting success. Pupils go on to Sherborne, Sherborne School for Girls and other Independent Senior Schools. There is a discount for Service families who have more than one child at the School.

DOR

Thornlow School

(Founded 1872)

101 Buxton Road,
Weymouth,
Dorset DT4 9PR
Tel: 01305 782977 Fax: 01305 778403

Heads: Mr D H Crocker, CertEd
Mrs J D Crocker, BA, PGCE
Type: Co-educational Independent Day and
Boarding School
Age range: 4-16. Boarders from 7-16
No. of pupils enrolled as at 1.9.94: 162
Junior: Boys 42 Girls 18; Senior: Boys 78 Girls 24
Fees per annum: Day: £2115-£3480
Boarding: £6540-£7635

Religious denomination: Inter-denominational

Member of: ISAI, ISIS

Curriculum: At Thornlow each pupil is an individual which encourages a high academic standard and excellent GCSE results. Scholarships are offered to pupils entering Years 7 and 9. Our broad curriculum includes separate sciences and Dyslexic support.

There are a wide range of after school activities including ACF and D of E scheme. We have a 25m heated indoor swimming pool and our site, overlooking Portland Harbour, enables pupils to sail and canoe.

Junior Boarders are accommodated in the main school and the Senior Boarding House is on site. During 1995 the boarding accommodation has been refurbished to a high standard. Escorts are provided to and from airports.

Thornlow has time for everyone - pupils and parents.

Entry requirements: Headmaster/ Headmistress interview and school report.

Somerset

SOM

Edgarley Hall

(Millfield Junior School)

(Founded 1946)

Edgarley Hall, Glastonbury, Somerset BA6 8LD
Tel: 01458 832446 Fax: 01458 833679

Head: Mr Richard Smyth, MA, PGCE
Type: Preparatory School
Age range: 8-13
No. of pupils enrolled as at 1.1.95: 440
Boarding: 162 Boys 92 Girls; Day: 100 Boys 86 Girls
Fees per term: Day: £2060; Boarding: £3150

Religious denomination: Inter-denominational

Average size of class: 13

Teacher/pupil ratio: 1:8

Curriculum: Pupils are taught mainly by their class teacher until the age of nine. The curriculum remains broad with all pupils studying Art, Craft, Technology and Music throughout the school. Specialist staff and small teaching groups ensure that pupils learn at a pace that suits their individual needs.

Excellent Scholarship and Common Entrance results are gained to Millfield and other well known senior schools.

Specialist help is provided by our Language Development Centre for pupils with specific learning difficulties.

Entry requirements: Entry by interview with Headmaster and a report from present school OR by bursary examination set in January.

Academic and leisure facilities offered: Edgarley provides staff and pupils with excellent modern facilities and equipment for academic work, music, drama, sport and over 90 clubs and activities flourish.

Edgarley Hall is a fully co-educational preparatory school set in 60 acres of beautiful countryside at the foot of Glastonbury Tor.

The Millfield Charitable Trust exists for the education of pupils and associated activities.

Perrott Hill School

(Founded 1946)

North Perrott,
Crewkerne,
Somerset TA18 7SL
Tel: 01460 72051 Fax: 01460 78246

Headmaster: J E A Barnes, BA, PGCE
Type: Preparatory School
Age range: 3-13+. Boarders from 7
No. of pupils enrolled as at 1.1.95: 129
103 Boys 26 Girls
Fees per annum:
Day: £1575-£5265; Boarding: £7320

Religious affiliation: Church of England

Member of: IAPS

Curriculum: Perrott Hill School is set in the heart of the Somerset countryside, and is serviced by excellent road and rail networks. The School is co-educational, with boarding and day pupils. Small classes and excellent academic facilities are reflected by an outstanding scholarship record, and 100% placement of pupils in their first choice public schools for the past five years. Recent developments include a CDT/Art Centre, Computer Centre and a Pre-Preparatory Department. Scholarships for academic, musical and all-round ability are offered annually. Games and extra curricular activities utilising 25 acres of space ensures a positive framework for a happy and successful educational environment.

The Perrott Hill School Charitable Trust exists to provide high quality education for boys and girls.

Sidcot School

(Founded 1808)

Winscombe,
North Somerset BS25 1PD
Tel: 01934 843102 Fax: 01934 844181

Head: Christopher Greenfield, MA, MEd
Type: Independent Co-educational Day and
Boarding School
Age range: 9-18
No of pupils enrolled as at 1.1.95: 390
Junior: 35 Boys 27 Girls
Senior: 121 Boys 107 Girls
Sixth Form: 51 Boys 50 Girls
Fees per annum:
Day: from £4101; Boarding: £9282

Religious affiliation: Quaker

Member of: BSA, SHMIS, GBA

Curriculum: Sidcot follows the National Curriculum, plus wider options such as Latin and Drama. At Key Stage Four the School offers alternatives as well as the National Curriculum. Music, drama and creativity are special strengths, but science and mathematics are also strong. A new science block has been built, and a sports centre and library have also been completed. Horse riding and many other activities are offered.

Entry requirements: Test and interview or Common Entrance.

The aim of Sidcot School Charitable Trust is the education of children in a Quaker and caring environment.

Wiltshire

WIL

Calder House School

(Founded 1995)

*Colerne, Nr Bath,
Wiltshire SN14 8BN
Tel: 01225 742329 Fax: 01225 742329*

Principal: Mrs Sandra Agombar, BA(Hons)
Type: Co-educational Day School
Age range: 5-13
No of pupils enrolled as at 1.5.95: New school, potential maximimum 50
Fees per annum: £5100-£5700

Religious affiliation: Inter-denominational

New school, awaiting accreditation by Council for the Registration of Schools Teaching Dyslexic Pupils (Crested) and the British Dyslexia Association.

Curriculum: Calder House is a new preparatory school, opened in 1995 by the founders and proprietors of Calder House School, London. It is run in the way that has proved so successful for the London School.

Calder House is suitable for children of average ability, but uneven achievement, who learn best with structured teaching in a supportive and non-competitive environment. Pupils follow the National Curriculum, and enjoy a full range of school activities. They are taught in small classes with a high staff:pupil ratio. Any specialist remedial help required is incorporated into the school day.

Entry requirements: Interview and school assessment.

Leaden Hall School

(Founded 1947)

*70 The Close,
Salisbury, Wiltshire SP1 2EP
Tel: 01722 334700 Fax: 01722 410575*

Head: Mrs Diana Watkins, MA
Type: Preparatory School
Age range: 3-12+. Boarders from 7
No. of pupils enrolled as at 1.9.94: 184 Girls
Fees per term: Day: Nursery £740, Pre-Prep £965,
Prep £1160, Boarding: £2080

Religious denomination: Christian

Member of: IAPS, BSA

Leaden Hall provides a single sex education for girls. Our high academic standards prepare children for the County 11+ examination, Common Entrance and Scholarships. We aim to give all girls self-confidence balanced with an awareness of others and a belief in themselves. The Cathedral Close provides a stimulating and attractive environment in which to learn.

We believe that boarding should be comfortable, fun and stimulating. After-school and weekend activities are action packed to allow the children to experience the very best in school life.

Full, weekly and day boarding options give parents the flexibility to enable their daughters to take part in the many extra-curricular activities.

Entry requirements: Interview/assessment.

A Registered Charity which exists to provide education for children.

Institutions offering Further Education appear in their own Section

---

Marlborough College

(Founded 1843)

Marlborough, Wiltshire SN8 1PA
Tel: 01672 515511 (Ext 297) Fax: 01672 516234

Principal: E J H Gould, MA
Type: Co-educational Boarding and Day School
Age range: 13-18
No. of students enrolled as at 1.9.94: 525 Boys 271 Girls
Sixth Form: 217 Boys 151 Girls
Teacher/student ratio: 1:8
Nature of tuition: Lectures, classes, small groups and one-to-one
Fees per term: Day Pupil: £2850; Tuition and Boarding accommodation: £4040

Member of: HMC, SHA

Courses: A choice of 23 A level courses is offered.

- Art, Design, Theatre Studies

- Business Studies

- Classical Civilisation, Latin, Greek

- English

- French, German, Spanish, Russian

- Geography

- History of Art, Medieval History, Modern History, Politics

- Mathematics, Further Mathematics

- Music

- Physics, Chemistry, Biology

In addition there are two AS level courses (English Language and French) and UCLES courses in Arabic, Mandarin Chinese, Computing and Japanese. There are non-examined General Studies for all Sixth Form students and all pupils study at least three A levels. 19 of the above subjects are taught at GCSE and details of the Lower School Curriculum may be obtained from the Senior Admissions Tutor.

Examinations offered including Boards:
A levels (O & C, London, AEB, Oxford Local); AS levels (same Boards), UCLES; Associated Board of Music. GCSE: SEG, NEAB, MEG, SMP, ULEAC.

Marlborough is a fully co-educational boarding and day school catering for some 800 pupils. The College is beautifully situated in 180 acres of its own grounds, one hour west of London, within easy reach of the M4 and Inter-City connections.

Accommodation: Marlborough has 14 boarding Houses. Girls entering the Lower School may choose from four houses, while boys have a choice of ten. A girl Sixth Form entrant will join one of the four girls' Houses, or one of the five that are mixed at Sixth Form level only; a boy will join either one of the five mixed or one of the five boys' Houses.

Facilities: teaching areas are generally modern and include brand new chemistry labs, science lecture rooms and a £1.2 million language centre. Sports are well catered for including two full size astro-turf pitches, an indoor sports hall with five cricket nets, a Gymnasium as well as indoor and outdoor swimming pools.

- 34 sports are played

- Over 40 Learned and recreational societies are available.

Entry requirements and procedure: for Upper School entrants applications should usually be made by the middle of the October prior to GCSE/KS4 exams, as scholarship and entrance assessments are held in the November. Scholarship applicants for Lower School entry must be received by the middle of January and Common Entrance applications should usually be received by 1 March.

There are Academic, Art and Music scholarships at all levels and General Awards based on all-round ability are available for Lower School entrants. For all candidates, the assessment comprises interview, written papers and school report. Places are offered to successful Sixth Form candidates conditional on their achieving the required number of grades C or better in GCSE/KS4. Lower School entrants must reach the accepted standard in the entrance exam.

Intending applicants and their parents are always welcome to visit Marlborough and to discuss the entry procedures in detail.

Marlborough is a charitable foundation of the Anglican Church based upon a commitment to achieving the best through active work and an independence of mind within respect for the community, its people and rules.

For further details please contact: The Senior Admissions Tutor, Marlborough College, Marlborough, Wiltshire SN8 1PS. Tel: 01672 512684 or 01672 515511. Fax: 01672 516234.

Pinewood School

(Founded 1875)

*Bourton,
Swindon,.
Wiltshire SN6 8HZ
Tel: 01793 782205 Fax: 01793 783476*

Headmaster: Mr H G C Boddington, MA(Oxon)
Type: Preparatory School
Age range: 4-13. Boarding from 8.
No. of pupils enrolled as at 1.5.95: 180
Junior: 121 Boys 59 Girls
Fees per annum:
Day: £2550-£5760; Boarding £7560

Religious affiliation: Church of England

Member of: IAPS, ISIS

Curriculum: Pinewood offers the advantages of a small School (average class size is 14) with outstanding facilities, set in splendid rural surroundings. The School is divided between day children and boarders: both boys and girls flourish in the happy, caring atmosphere. Recently, a major building programme has produced a new music school, art rooms and workshop, as well as classrooms, kitchens and changing rooms. Academic results are impressive, with Scholarships gained to senior schools and individual attention offered to the weaker pupil. A wide range of games and activities mean that every child is able to find an area of enjoyment and, hopefully, of excellence. Pinewood also has a thriving Pre-prep department, taking children from the age of 4, with its own purpose-built accomodation.

Entry requirements: Assessment at 7+. Interview with Headmaster.

Pinewood School Ltd, which is a registered charity, exists to provide high quality education for boarders and local children.

Don't forget to read the articles at the beginning of the book – they may save you a lot of time and trouble

A list of useful Educational Associations appears at the back of this book

Salisbury Cathedral School

(Founded 1091 AD)

The Old Palace,
1 The Close, Salisbury,
Wiltshire SP1 2EQ
Tel: 01722 322652

Head: C J A Helyer, CertEd, ACP
Type: Preparatory and Choir School:
Pre-preparatory. All Co-ed.
Age range: 3½-13. Boarders from 8-13
No. of pupils enrolled as at 10.1.95:
Pre-Prep: 88 Boys 42 Girls;
Junior: 107 Boys 65 Girls
Fees per annum:
Day: Pre-Prep £2910, Prep £5610; Boarding: £7440

Religious denomination: Church of England

Member of: IAPS, CSA

Curriculum: The majority of pupils work towards the Common Entrance and 13+ Scholarship assessments, although a limited number of pupils do take 11+ and 12+ assessments for local schools. The music department is particularly strong and a number of children obtain music awards at senior independent schools. Drama is included in the curriculum for all pupils.

Entry requirements: All pupils are required to do assessments in English, maths and reading, and reports from a pupil's present school are considered most valuable.

The Cathedral School Charitable Trust exists to provide an education for boys and girls.

Looking for a school somewhere else in Britain? Why not consult *Which School?* now in its 70th edition, also published by John Catt Educational Ltd

---

Sandroyd

(Founded 1888)

Rushmore, Tollard Royal,
Salisbury, Wiltshire SP5 5QD
Tel: 01725 516264 Fax: 01725 516441

Head: Mr M J Hatch, MA(Oxon)
Type: Boys Preparatory School
Age range: 7-13. Boarders from 7
No of pupils enrolled as at 1.5.95: 137
Fees per annum:
Day: £7200; Boarding: £8610

Religious affiliation: Church of England

Member of: IAPS, BSA

Sandroyd is set in uniquely beautiful parkland in Cranborne Chase. Primarily a boarding school, but with some day places, all boys benefit from modern accommodation in a secure, family environment.

Facilities include a well-equipped computer lab, Art/CDT centre, stables and an impressive indoor pool. There is coaching in a full range of team sports, with tuition in riding, shooting, squash and golf.

The boys are prepared for Scholarship and Common Entrance examinations to all leading public schools. Music, both choral and instrumental, is given a high priority and there is a specialist department for boys with particular learning difficulties.

Sandroyd School is a registered charity for the purpose of providing education.

Scholarships in areas
outside the South West

London

Clifton Lodge

(Founded 1979)

8 Mattock Lane, Ealing,
London W5 5BG
Tel: 0181 579 3662

Head: D.A.P. Blumlein, BA
Type: Boys' Preparatory School
Age range: 4-13.
No. of pupils enrolled as at 1.9.94:
Junior: 40 Boys; Senior/Sixth Form: 120 Boys
Fees per annum:
Day: £4100-£4600

Religious denomination: Christian

Choristerships: Boys who wish to join the choir as full choristers are entitled to choristerships on successful graduation. These choral scholarships are awarded to the value of one third of the basic fees, provided that parents make a commitment to 13+ and undertake to make the boy available when required. A chorister's duties never encroach on his academic programme or other essential asects of school life.

Further details available from the Headmaster.

Display Listings of Schools
in areas outside the South West

Berkshire

C h e a m Hawtreys

(Founded 1645)

Headley, Newbury, Berkshire RG19 8LD
Tel: 01635 268242 Fax: 01635 269345

Headmaster: Mr C C Evers, BA (Member of IAPS)
Type: Preparatory School
Age range: 7-13. Boarders from 8
No. of pupils enrolled as at 1.5.95: 165
Fees per annum: Day: £1970; Boarding: £2855

Religious affiliation: Church of England

Member of: ISIS

Curriculum: The Public Schools Scholarship and Common Entrance syllabus which complies with and exceeds National Curriculum requirements.

Examinations offered: Scholarship and Common Entrance to public schools.

Religious activities: Regular morning prayers. Sunday Services.

Scholarships, Exhibitions and Bursaries: Two Scholarships offered annually for up to 30% of fees. The Haughey Scholarship is for a boarder, the Governors' Scholarship is for either a boarder or a day boy. Examinations held late February or early March.

Location: Located in 80 acres of parkland on the borders of Berkshire and Hampshire, the School is easily accessible from both the M3 and M4. Ten minutes from Newbury and 15 minutes from Basingstoke it is just over an hour from West London and Bristol, and less from Oxford and Portsmouth. A coach service

to London is provided at the beginning and end of half-term and exeats.

Academic, sports, games and leisure facilities:
Academic: Small classes following the curriculum in all major subjects (including Latin). Up to three streams in the last three years. Most classrooms enjoy dedicated video facilities. Quiet library. Additional support unit available for those with learning difficulties. Thriving Music department (orchestra and two choirs, sound-proofed [almost!] percussion room), networked 30 station computer centre; good Art and Design centre.

Sports: Extensive playing fields. Large dedicated Sports Hall, heated outdoor pool, four all-weather hard tennis courts, golf course, squash court. Rugby, soccer, hockey and cross-country in winter terms; cricket, tennis, athletics and swimming in summer term. Basketball, judo, rifle shooting (including matches), badminton, short tennis, canoeing training and instruction. **Games and Leisure Facilities:** Climbing wall, adventure slide and obstacle course. Camping ground (summer term). 'Camps' – a wooded part of the 80 acre parkland site. Croquet lawn (summer term, 1st Form). Four separate play rooms/TV rooms for different year groups. Pool room. Modelling room. Tuck shop. Activities: Once a week, instead of games, there is a formal 'activities' period. Activities are also offered during an extended lunch break and in the evenings. Activities include cooking, craft, motor cycle maintenance, bridge and fly-tying among other things.

Boarding (approximately 80%). Comfortable, carpeted and curtained dormitories, separate first year boarding house (Benham House), run by the resident housemaster and his wife. The young boarders have breakfast in their house before joining the main school, and return to Benham for an evening drink and bedtime story. Four resident matrons and four resident tutors look after the welfare of the boarders upstairs and a system of Trust and Cooperation is inculcated in a relaxed atmosphere. Day Boys: day boys arrive in time for morning assembly (8.20 am) and are fully integrated into all school events. They return home after prep (approximately 6.30 pm). A mini-bus service is operated to Marlborough.

Cheam School Educational Trust, a registered charity, exists to foster excellence in education, awareness of others and development of the whole being.

Traditional Values
Modern Thinking
Education for the 21st Century

Pangbourne College

(Founded 1917)

*Pangbourne,
Near Reading,
Berkshire RG8 8LA
Tel: 01734 842101 Fax: 01734 845443*

Head: Mr Anthony Hudson, MA(Oxon), DipEd(London)
Type: Independent School
Age range: 11-18. Boarders from 11
No. of pupils enrolled as at 1.9.94: 390
Junior: 30 Boys; Senior: 360 Boys
Sixth Form: 125 Boys 6 girls
Fees per annum:
Junior (11-13): Day £5520, Boarding £7920
Senior (13-18): Day £7620, Boarding £10,860

Religious denomination: Church of England

Member of: HMC, SHMIS, ISIS, Boarding Schools Association

Pangbourne College is an independent HMC school devoted to providing the best possible education for individual strengths and abilities – borne out by pleasing academic results. There are 17 core and option subjects at GCSE and 20 A level choices.

Boys and girls can start from September 1996 at the age of 11. For two years, the youngest belong to the Junior School, with its own beautiful house surrounded by playing-fields, gardens and woods. Further admissions come at 13+ and to the Sixth Form, but all share fully in the splendid facilities of the main school. Set in fine grounds of 240 acres, the College boasts extensive facilities including Computer, Electronics and Science Laboratories and a Design Technology Centre. The fine new computerised Library forms part of the Academic Quadrangle. Adjacent buildings house the superb new Modern Languages Facility, a Geography teaching suite, Careers/Higher Education Resource Centre with CD-ROM database and dedicated Learning Support department and the Drake Centre, popular for performing arts. An extensive range of sports and games, pursued to the highest standards, is provided for by excellent facilities.

The newly-opened Social Centre provides a recreational and cultural resource for the largest Sixth Form in the history of the College.

Generous scholarship provision at all levels enhances a lively academic and artistic atmosphere. There are Academic, Music, Art, Technology and All-Rounders Awards of up to half fees.

Pangbourne College Ltd exists to provide an all-round education for boys and girls between the ages of 11 and 18 years.

BER

Queen Anne's School

(Founded 1894)

*6 Henley Road,
Caversham, Reading,
Berkshire RG4 0DX
Tel: 01734 471582 Fax: 01734 461498*

Headmistress: Mrs D. Forbes, MA (Oxon)
Type: Girls Independent Boarding and Day School
Age range: 11 - 18. Boarders from 11
No. of pupils enrolled as at 1.5.95:
Senior: 240 Sixth Form: 80
Fees per term: Day: £2300; Boarding: £3550

Religious denomination: Anglican

Member of: GSA, GBGSA

Curriculum: Queen Anne's offers an education of a high academic standard and based on Christian principles. There is a large Sixth Form operating on a tutorial system with over 90% of girls gaining University entrance. Six Scholarships (one of full tuition fees) are awarded each year and can be supplemented according to income. There are also Sixth Form Scholarships and Scholarships in Music (half fees) and Art.

There are excellent facilities for sport including a new indoor swimming pool and tennis and squash courts. There is a fine new Library, a new Modern Languages Block and a Performing Arts Centre was opened in June 1994.

Queen Anne's School is a registered charity, and exists to provide a high standard of education for girls.

Gloucestershire

Bredon School

(Founded 1962)

*Pull Court, Bushley,
Near Tewkesbury,
Gloucestershire GL20 6AH
Tel: 01684 293156*

Head: Mr C.E. Wheeler
Type: Independent Boarding and Day School
Age range: 5-18. Boarders from 7
No. of pupils enrolled as at 1.9.94:
Junior: 38 Boys 17 Girls;
Senior: 159 Boys 41 Girls; Sixth Form: 65
Fees per annum:
Day: £2250-£6300; Boarding £7740-£11,580

Religious denomination: Church of England

Member of: ISAI, BSA, The Dyslexia Association

Curriculum: Bredon is a co-educational independent school for 300 pupils with full and weekly boarders and day pupils. The main site, known as Pull Court, stands in attractive rural surroundings near the River Severn, on the Worcestershire and Gloucestershire boarders in an estate of 85 acres, which includes a school farm. The other site, accommodating the junior school and girls' boarding house, is at Sarn Hill Grange, in the village of Bushley, approximately one mile from Pull Court. The School follows the National Curriculum at all Key Stages and students will sit the National assessment tests at the appropriate stages. A primary or Preparatory education is offered from 5-10+. A Secondary education commences at 11+ with a Foundation Course to 13+, 16+ examination courses for the 14-15+ age range, and Advanced Courses at the Post-16 stage. At all stages, the requirements of the National Curriculum will be adhered to, including major assessments of pupil performance carried out at 7+, 11+ and 13+, including Standard Assessment Tests.

Entry requirements: There is no entrance examination, but an applicant is required to attend the School for interview with the Headmaster. Acceptance is subject to the result of the interview and to a satisfactory report from the pupil's Headmaster. Pupils are accepted from the age of 5; direct entry into all other year courses is acceptable, and can be arranged with the Headmaster.

Examinations offered: Pupils are prepared for GCSE, A and AS level, in a wide variety of subjects depending on individual ability. The School also offers a range of BTEC/GNVQ Foundation, Intermediate and Advanced programmes in Business, Leisure, Health and Social Care, Design and Manufacturing (Engineering), also NVQ Agriculture and Horticulture.

Academic and leisure facilities: Class size 6-15. Teacher/pupil ratio: 1:7. A Learning Support Centre gives specialist support and teaching for those experiencing learning difficulties. Bredon aims to provide a sound general education and, with this in view, has set out to: 1) Educate the whole pupil and not merely the academic side. 2) Help pupils achieve the academic standard of which they are capable, employing well- qualified staff, and operating in small classes. 3) Develop a pupil's character and interests. Excellent facilities exist in Craft, Design & Technology, Computer Studies, and a Farm Unit provides the basis for Agricultural Studies. The main School games are Rugby football, Cricket, Cross-Country, Athletics. On one afternoon a week, a wider choice is available, including Hockey, Weight-Training, Canoeing, Fencing, Soccer, Squash, Swimming, and a number of other minor sports. There is a flourishing Adventure Training/Outdoor Pursuits interest, which operates throughout the year, culminating in major expeditions. The School is an independent centre for the Duke of Edinburgh's Award Scheme. Numerous holiday activities are organised, which have included skiing and mountaineering in various European countries and Field Study trips.

GLO

Selwyn School

(Founded 1958)

*Matson House, Matson Lane,
Gloucester GL4 9DY
Tel: 01452 305663; Fax: 01452 385907*

Head: Miss L M Brown, BA, MA(Ed), CertEd
Type: Independent School
Age range: 3-18. Boarders 8-18
No of pupils enrolled as at 1.5.94: 300
Junior: 43 Boys 100 Girls; Senior: 130 Girls
Sixth Form: 27 Girls
Fees per annum:
Day: £2055-£4800; Boarding: £6060-£8430
Sixth Form: Day £4800; Boarding £8430

Religious affiliation: Anglican but all faiths and denominations welcome

Member of: GSA

Curriculum: The curriculum is broad and balanced. Enriched national curriculum. Strong drama and arts. Junior School is subject based. Introduces French. Wide GCSE options. Choice of A and AS levels from 15 subjects. Excellent standards. Regular entries to Universities. Sports fields on site. Specialist accommodation. EFL and Dyslexia Departments. Over 35 extra-curricular activities. Individual attention. Good discipline. Affordable fees. Small homely boarding house. Flexible admissions. Anglican foundation and chaplain, but all faiths welcome.

Entry requirements: Entrance test, interview and reference from school. Academic, music and sporting scholarships.

Hampshire

Lord Wandsworth College

(Founded 1912)

Long Sutton,
Hook, Hampshire RG29 1TB
Tel: 01256 862482 Fax: 01256 862563

Head: Mr G. de W. Waller, MA, MSc
Type: Independent, Boarding & Day School,
Boys and Sixth Form Girls
Age range: 11-18. Boarders from 11-18
No. of pupils enrolled as at 1.9.95: 475
Junior: 82 Boys Senior: 348 Boys 45 Girls
Sixth Form: 110 Boys 45 Girls
Fees per annum as at 1.9.95:
Day: £7096-£7418,   Boarding: £9086-£9488

Religious denomination: Inter-denominational

Member of: HMC, GBA, SHMIS

Curriculum: 11-16 broadly follows National
Curriculum with Latin, Classical
Civilisation, Spanish and German also
offered as options. There is a wide range of
A levels in the Sixth Form. Extra curricular
activities are particularly encouraged with
excellent facilities on offer in a beautiful,
rural setting.

Entry requirements: Own test at 11+,
Common Entrance at 13+, interview,
reference and test for Sixth Form.

The Lord Wandsworth Foundation supports
up to 20 pupils a year and these are
selected by a separate testing procedure.
Foundationers are sons/daughters of
widowers, widows or single parents.

Lord Wandsworth College Charitable Trust
exists to provide the highest possible
standards of education to foundationers and
fee payers alike.

St Swithun's School

(Founded 1844)

Alresford Road,
Winchester,
Hampshire SO21 1HA
Tel: 01962 861316
Fax: 01962 841874

Headmistress: Dr H L Harvey, BSc, PhD (London)
Type: Girls' Independent School
Age range: 11-18.
Boarders from 11.
No. of pupils enrolled as at 1.9.94:
458 (including Sixth Form: 95 Girls)
Fees per annum:
Day: £6465; Boarding: £10,695

Religious denomination: Church of England

Member of: GBGSA, GSA, BSA

St Swithun's School (Winchester), a
Registered Charity, exists to provide
education for girls, both Day and Boarding,
aged 11-18 years.

The School was founded in 1884 in the city of
Winchester and moved in 1931 to its present
fine site on the Downs to the east of the city,
about a mile from its centre.

The majority of girls enter the Senior
School between the ages of 11 and 13 years
by means of the Common Entrance
Examination for Independent Schools, but

girls are accepted at other ages, including the Sixth Form, subject to satisfactory tests.

A flexible, broadly-based education is offered, enabling girls to develop their potential. 19 subjects are available at GCSE of which English Language and Literature, a modern Foreign Language, Mathematics and at least one Physical Science subject are compulsory. The selection of others is made on an individual basis with an emphasis on breadth of course as well as future career prospects. In the Sixth Form, girls are offered a free choice of 24 subjects and all follow to A level a challenging and wide-ranging General Course.

The School flourishes in a way appropriate to the present day, but is glad to be firmly rooted in its fine traditions. In attitude it largely reflects the changes and relaxations found in any modern institution or community. Within a framework of easier discipline, there is a remarkably friendly and caring atmosphere in the School.

Institutions offering Further Education appear in their own Section

---

HAM

Stroud School

(Founded 1926)

*Highwood House,
Highwood Lane,
Romsey,
Hampshire SO51 9ZH
Tel/Fax: 01794 513231*

Head: Mr A J L Dodds, MA(Cantab) (Member of IAPS)
Type: Co-educational Preparatory School
Age range: 3-13
No of pupils enrolled as at 1.5.95: 250
185 Boys (17 are 11+) 65 Girls (4 are 11+)
Fees per annum: £1560-£5529

Religious affiliation: Church of England

Member of: IAPS, ISJC

Curriculum: Boys and girls are prepared for the Common Entrance Examination and for scholarships to independent senior and grammar schools.

Entry requirements: Interview.

Stroud is a co-educational day preparatory school with a kindergarten and pre-preparatory department.

The School aims to provide a full all-round education offering a wide range of opportunities and activities in a relaxed, but disciplined, atmosphere, enabling children to realise their full potential.

Children are prepared for Common Entrance and Scholarships to a wide range of independent and Grammar Schools. Academically and on the games field, Stroud has an excellent record.

Situated in an attractive rural setting within easy reach of Winchester, Southampton, Salisbury and the New Forest, the School stands in 20 acres of grounds which include playing fields, solar heated swimming pool, tennis courts, hard playing areas and gardens.

Hertfordshire

St Christopher School

(Founded 1915)

*Letchworth,
Hertfordshire SG6 3JZ
Tel: 01462 679301 Fax: 01462 481578*

Headmaster: Mr Colin Reid, MA
Type: Co-educational Boarding and Day School
Age range: 2½-18. Boarders from 7:
Half of the senior school are boarders
No. of pupils enrolled as at 2.1.95:
Junior: 84 Boys 47 Girls;
Senior: 205 Boys 137 Girls
Sixth Form: 43 Boys 42 Girls
Average size of class: 16; Teacher/Pupil ratio: 1: 7
Fees per term:
Day: £1256; Boarding: £2815;
Senior Day: £1992; Senior Boarding: £3517

Location: One mile from A1(M) and 35 minutes from Kings Cross.

Religious affiliation: Non-denominational

Member of: GBA

Curriculum: The core areas of the National Curriculum are covered with all pupils continuing with Physics, Chemistry and Biology to Double Certificate Level at the GCSE. Foreign Languages have a strongly practical emphasis with all pupils paying at least one visit to our exchange schools in France and/or Germany in years II, III and IV. The creative arts and technology are particularly encouraged and the facilities are available and staffed at weekends. Internationalist and green values are fostered. The diet is vegetarian.

Entry requirements: Entry for boarders is usually at age 11 with some joining at 9 and others at 13. Decisions are made in the light of interview, school reports and informal tests, usually conducted on the day of interview. We look for an ability to respond to the spirit and opportunities of St Christopher. Direct entrants to the Sixth Form have to show that they are ready to follow a 3 A/AS level programme. The School provides for children of average to

outstanding ability aiming to help everyone achieve their full potential.

Examinations offered: GCSE (MEG, NEG, SEG); GCE A and AS levels (Oxford & Cambridge, JMB, AEB) in 17 subjects.

Destination and career prospects of leavers: Almost all leavers go on to a course in further or higher education.

Boarding: Half the pupils aged over 11 are boarders. The younger ones live with houseparents in a warm domestic setting while Sixth formers have student style rooms.

Academic and sports facilities: The School has all the usual specialist rooms and science laboratories with particularly fine Theatre, Music and Arts Centres added in recent years. As one of the pilot schools of Education 2000 it has pioneered major developments in information technology, and two computer networks link the library and all the teaching areas. We complement academic study with learning through experience. There is a strong emphasis on Outdoor Pursuits (with all pupils learning to canoe, sail and rock climb), on service to the whole community and on self-government through which pupils learn both how to put forward their own ideas and listen to those of others.

Values: The School is an unusually tolerant community, recognising and caring for all as individuals. There is no compulsory worship so people of different religions and of none feel equally at home. There is a significant period of silence in every assembly.

Long-term aims: St Christopher has long been noted for its success in developing lifelong self-confidence. The School is informal (there is no uniform and all children and adults are called by their first names); at the same time it is purposeful and challenging of mind, body and spirit. We aim for our young people to develop an effective competence, a social conscience, moral courage, a sense of initiative, the capacity for friendship and a true zest for life.

St Christopher School is a registered charity providing education for 3 to 18 year olds, with boarders from age 7.

Looking for a school somewhere else in Britain? Why not consult *Which School?* now in its 70th edition, also published by John Catt Educational Ltd

---

Kent

KEN

Breaside Preparatory School

(Founded 1950)

*41-43 Orchard Road,
Bromley, Kent BR1 2PR
Tel: 0181 460 0916*

Headmaster: Mr Neil G Murray, DipEd, ManDip, Member of ISAI
Type: Independent Co-educational Preparatory and Pre-Prep
Age range: 3-11
No. of pupils enrolled as at 1.1.95: 208
Fees per annum: Day: £1590-£3165

Religious affiliation: Interdenominational

Curriculum: Breaside gives children a happy, confident start to school life. Well-taught, they leave at 11 for the leading London schools. While at Breaside children learn to live up to high standards of work, behaviour and concern for others.

There is ample space on site. Classes average about 16 in size and are taken by experienced teachers. The National Curriculum and the requirements of Senior Schools are guides to the School syllabus. French is taught from 6+.

The lower classes are organised separately and have breaks and lunches away from the older children. The under fives have their own purpose built classrooms and play area.

There are also two pre-Schools, open 50 weeks a year, from 8am to 6pm Monday to Friday, associated with Breaside.

Entry requirements: Entry is by interview and assessment where appropriate. Scholarships are offered at 7+.

KEN

Duke of York's Royal Military School

(Founded 1803)

Dover, Kent CT15 5EQ
Tel: 01304 245024

Head: Col G H Wilson, BA, MEd
(Member of SHMIS)
Type: Independent Co-educational Boarding School
Age range: 11+-18+
No. of pupils enrolled as at 1.9.94: 476
Junior (11-13): 102 Boys 23 Girls
Senior (13+-16): 224 Boys 20 Girls;
Sixth Form: 99 Boys 8 Girls
Fees per term: Boarding: £300

Religious denomination: Church of England
(Roman Catholic & Free Church welcome).

Member of: GBA, BSA, ISIS

Curriculum: A broad based common core
of subjects, in line with the National
Curriculum, leading to 7 to 11 GCSE entries
per candidate in year 11.

Sixth Form courses provide for a range of
GCE subjects. Three A levels with General
Studies at A or AS level is the norm.
Alternatively, BTEC National Diploma
course in Engineering or GNVQ level 3
course in Business are available. The Sixth
Form study at least one European language.

Entry requirements: Examinations in
English, Mathematics and good
Headteacher's report. Four years service
in HM Forces by either parent.

KEN

St David's College

(Founded 1926)

Beckenham Road,
West Wickham
Kent BR4 0QS
Tel: 0181 777 5852 Fax: 0181 777 9549
E-mail:100545, 3042 Compuserve.Com

Principals: Mrs P A Johnson, CertEd, FRGS
(Member of NAHT)
Mrs F V Schove (ISAI); Mrs A Wagstaff, BA(Hons)Lond
Type: Co-educational Day School
Age range: 4-11
No of pupils enrolled as at 1.5.95: 197
Junior: 104 Boys 93 Girls
Fees per annum: £2415-£2565;

Religious affiliation: Inter-denominational

Member of: ISAI, ISIS

Curriculum: St David's College offers
a wide and varied academic and sporting
curriculum. At the age of 11 pupils are
entered for the independent schools' entrance
examinations, as well as for the London
Boroughs of Bexley, Bromley and Sutton
selective examinations, with outstanding
results. Kent Grammar School places are
also achieved each year.

After-school activities include Ballet
and French Club. Pupils also have the
opportunity to learn Speech and Drama,
Clarinet, Piano, Recorder and Violin.

St David's is situated in six acres of beautiful
playing fields and grounds. The main sports
are athletics, cricket and football.

Entry requirements: Entrance is by test and
interview.

London

(Founded 1979)

8 Mattock Lane, Ealing, London W5 5BG
Tel: 0181 579 3662

Head: D.A.P. Blumlein, BA
Type: Boys' Preparatory School
Age range: 4-13. *No. of pupils enrolled as at 1.9.94:*
Junior: 40 Boys; Senior/Sixth Form: 120 boys
Fees per annum: Day: £4100-£4600

Religious denomination: Christian

Clifton Lodge is a school that stands for standards: standards of proper behaviour and all that that embraces in attitudes to others and standards of personal achievement of any sort and we believe that boys want to be a success in life. This they can only obtain by hard work, confidence in their own ability and a properly disciplined approach, whatever the activity. Clifton Lodge seeks at all times to impart these values.

The School is geared to give much individual attention, with boys being able to work at their own level, enabling them to realise their own potential.

The curriculum is based on the need to prepare boys for entry to Public School at 13+ through the Common Entrance Examination, Public School Scholarships or other equivalent examinations, and Clifton Lodge is justifiably proud of its excellent record of success in these. Whereas this provides the core of the academic programme, nevertheless we consider it essential to educate all pupils as broadly as possible and much time is also given to Music, Sport and Drama, these avenues providing boys with valuable opportunities to develop further talents and to build up their self-confidence.

The school is of Christian denomination and the daily assembly, attended by the whole community, is based around these ideals.

Choristerships to the value of one third of the basic fees are available for singing boys.

We believe that the combination of these values, the emphasis put on self-discipline, and the healthy encouragement to achieve success both within and without the classroom are essential ingredients for any boy's future happiness and fulfillment in life.

Emanuel School

(Founded 1594)

Battersea Rise,
London SW11 1HS
Tel: 0181 870 4171 Fax: 0181 875 0267

Head: Mr Tristram Jones-Parry, MA
Type: Independent School
Age range: 10-18
No of pupils enrolled as at 1.5.95: 709
Junior: 202 Boys (Girls to be admitted into the
First Form from September 1996)
Senior: 379 Boys
Sixth Form: 128 Boys (Girls to be admitted into Sixth
Form from September 1995)
Fees per annum:
Day: £4026-£4326; Sixth Form: £4326

Religious affiliation: Church of England

Member of: HMC

Emanuel School, near Wandsworth Common, is an independent school for boys aged 10-18, although from September 1995 girls will be admitted into the Sixth Form and from September 1996 girls will be admitted at 10+ and 11+. Assisted places and scholarships are available at 11+, 13+ and Sixth Form.

The introduction of girls is, in fact, a return to the co-educational origins of Emanuel School dating back to 1594. However, the new students will not find the school weighed down by tradition. A new Sixth Form Centre opened last year, new changing rooms are currently being built for the school's swimming pool and the existing library is being completely refurbished and computerised over the next few months.

Emanuel continues to produce impressive academic results, with last year's A level pass rate just below 90%, and eleven subjects achieving 100% success, including key subjects like English, Maths and French.

There is also a wide range of extra-curricular activities on offer: December's production of 'The Taming of the Shrew' played to packed houses, the Emanuel rugby players returned undefeated from last summer's tour of Canada and the Boat Club enjoyed similar success in South Africa in February.

WC

International School of London

(Founded 1972)

139 Gunnersbury Avenue,
London W3 8LG
Tel: 0181 992 5823 Fax: 0181 993 7012

Headmaster: Mr Richard Hermon, MA
Type: International Co-educational
Independent Day School
Age range: 4-18
No. of pupils enrolled as at 1.5.95:
Junior: 40 Boys 30 Girls; Senior: 50 Boys 42 Girls
Sixth Form: 18 Boys 9 Girls
Fees per annum:
Day: £5190-£7890; Sixth Form: £8340

Member of: European Council of International Schools, London International Schools' Association, Association of Heads of Independent Schools.

Curriculum: The programme from nursery to GCSE follows English lines, but special consideration is given to native languages other than English, such as Arabic, Danish, French, Portuguese, Spanish, Japanese and Italian. Where necessary, English is also taught as a second language (ESL). The International Baccalaureate programme is offered in the Sixth Form.

Entry requirements: Previous schools' reports plus tests where appropriate. Non-English

speakers are assessed largely on reports and their language level is screened.

Examinations offered: GCSE (ULEAC, with some NEAB and MEG syllabuses), IGCSE, the International Baccalaureate, of which ISL is the pioneering school in London.

The School has a spacious playground as well as a Nursery playground and is an enclave of Gunnersbury Park, whose sports fields it uses. Indoor sports facilities are in the building for younger children or at the nearby Brentford Leisure Centre for seniors. Though easily accessible from Central London, the School provides door-to-door transport for most London areas.

A list of useful Educational Associations appears at the back of this book

SWF

L'Ecole des Petits

(Founded 1977)

*2 Hazlebury Road,
London SW6 2NB
Tel: 0171 371 8350*

Head: Mrs Mirella Otten, CAP
Type: Independent Bilingual Pre-Primary School
Age range: 2½-6
No of pupils enrolled as at 1.5.95: 120
Fees per term:
Full Day: £910- £990; Part Day: £670

whilst following a structured curriculum.

The school caters for children who progress on to both the French and English educational system. It promotes a bilingual atmosphere with an international flavour that prepares its children for the demands of today's modern world, whilst retaining a sense of joy combined with traditional family values.

Entry requirements: Interview with parents.

Religious affiliation: All denominations welcome

Member of: ISIS

L'Ecole des Petits aims to provide an education that enhances early learning skills in a controlled environment of small classes. It has a warm and friendly atmosphere that encourages its pupils to express themselves

The Montessori House

(Founded 1984)

5 Princes Avenue, Muswell Hill, London N10 3LS
Tel: 0181 444 4399

Head: Mrs Nicola Forsyth, AMI Dip
Type: Montessori School
Age range: 2-5
No of pupils enrolled as at 1.5.95: 30 Boys 33 Girls
Fees per annum: £1467-£3417

Religious affiliation: None

Member of: Registered AMI Montessori School

The Montessori House, Muswell Hill, is a high quality Montessori school. All the classrooms are equipped to the highest standard and there are no correspondence or part-time trained teachers.

At two years old children can join a class especially designed for such young children and continue on to a full morning. Later, they can stay for a home-cooked lunch followed by play in the large, secure garden. Eventually, at around four years, children stay until 3 pm which includes cookery, ballet and woodwork.

A proper Montessori environment gives children confidence in themselves and their abilities and, even more importantly, self motivation. As a result, children leaving at five are expected to reach a good standard of reading, writing and basic maths.

The school has a small pre-prep department for children from 5-7 years.

SWA

NWC

Miss Morleys' Nursery School

(Founded 1966)

Fountain Court Club Room,
Buckingham Palace Road,
London SW1
Tel: 0171 730 5797

Head: Mrs Christopher Spence
Type: Nursery School
Age range: 2½-5
No of pupils enrolled as at 1.5.95: 45
20 Boys 25 Girls
Fees per annum: £520-£650

Religious affiliation: All denominations

Miss Morleys is a school with a happy and relaxed atmosphere in which the children can make an excellent start to school life with elementary schooling, companionship, fun with care and control. The curriculum includes many art and musical activities thus occupying the children in interesting and varied ways during their hours with us.

The Royal School, Hampstead

(Founded 1855)

65 Rosslyn Hill,
London NW3 5UD
Tel: 0171 794 7708

Principal: Mrs C A Sibson, BA(Oxon)
Type: Girls' Independent Boarding and Day School
Age range: 4-18. Boarders from 7
No. of pupils enrolled as at 31.1.95:
Junior: 75 Girls; Senior: 90 Girls
Fees per term:
Day: £985-£1150; Boarding: £1984- £2734;
Weekly Boarding: £2025-£2534;
Sixth Form Day: £1150; Boarding: £2734;

Religious affiliation: Anglican
(other religions welcome)

The School was founded on its present site in 1855. The patron is HRH Princess Alexandra, the Hon Lady Ogilvy, GVCO. Today, the School is a small independent boarding and day school for girls. The School's curriculum includes the core subjects leading to GCSE, AS and A level examinations and is compatible with the National School Curriculum. It also includes two foreign languages and the combined sciences. There is a well qualified staff with a low pupil to teacher ratio.

Entry requirements: Entry to both the Senior and Junior departments is by interview and previous school reports. An entrance test is taken when applicable. Scholarships are available at 11 years, and for the Sixth Form.

Examinations offered: GCSE, AS, A levels, Pitmans and RSA.

The School is situated in pleasant and spacious surroundings. It has comfortable modern boarding accommodation and a large garden. There are excellent sports facilities. The School is close to London's major educational, cultural and recreational centres which are visited regularly. There is a large car park which facilitates the arrival and departure of pupils. The School was founded in the Christian tradition but girls of all faiths are welcome. An assembly is held most mornings.

The Royal School Hampstead is a registered charity which exists to provide a sound and broad-based education which prepares girls both to meet and cope with the challenges of the 1990s.

Sinclair House School

(Founded 1989)

159 Munster Road,
Fulham,
London SW6 6DA
Tel: 0171 736 9182

Head: Mrs E A Sinclair House, BA, Cert Ed Psy, PGC Ed, Cert Psychol (Member of BPS)
Type: Montessori Nursery and Pre-Preparatory School
Age range: 2½-8
No. of pupils enrolled as at 1.5.95: 60
Fees per annum: £1200-£3600

Member of: AIMS

Curriculum: Sinclair House School provides a traditional education with plenty of outdoor activity. English and Mathematics are taught individually; History, Geography, Science, Technology and French in class groups. Children participate in swimming, music, drama, gymnastics, trampolining, short tennis, hockey, football, athletics and cricket; painting, pottery and craftwork.

Entry requirements: Interview and trial day.

Sydenham High School GPDST

(Founded 1877)

19 Westwood Hill,
London SE26 6BL
Tel: 0181 778 8737 Fax: 0181 776 8830

Head: Mrs Geraldine Baker, BSc, FZS
Type: Girls' Independent Day School
Age range: 4-18
No. of pupils enrolled as at 1.9.94:
Junior: 240; Senior: 460; Sixth Form: 90
Fees per term: Junior: £1140; Senior: £1476

Religious denomination: Non-denominational

Member of: GPDST, GSA, ISIS, GBGSA, SHA

Curriculum: The school provides a broad, balanced education that fosters confidence through success.

Academic standards are very high. Girls are able to make a free choice at GCSE and A level from a very full range of subjects on offer. Music and Drama are vital elements of the school curriculum and extra curricular plays and concerts are frequent. 93% of students proceed to degree courses.

An attractive blend of Victorian buildings and purpose-built accommodation, the School provides excellent facilities, which include separate Technology and Sixth Form centres and a new Sports Hall. A full range of sport is offered both at school and at the National Stadium at Crystal Palace. The School is conveniently reached by public transport.

Entry requirements: Entry is normally at 4, 7, 11 and 16. Occasional places become available at other levels.

Sydenham High School, as a member of the Girls' Public Day School Trust, provides an excellent education for pupils of a wide range of ability. Registered Charity No. 1026057.

Middlesex

St David's School

(Founded 1716)

Church Road, Ashford,
Middlesex TW15 3DZ
Tel: 01784 252494 Fax: 01784 248652

Headmistress: Mrs Judith G Osborne, BA
(Member of GSA)
Type: Independent Girls Day and Boarding School
Age range: 3-18. Boarders from 8
No. of pupils enrolled as at 1.5.95:
Junior: 154; Senior: 237; Sixth Form: 32
Fees per annum:
Day: £4950, Boarding: Weekly £8100, Full £8595
Sixth Form: Day £4950;
Boarding: Weekly £8100, Full £8595

Religious affiliation: Church of England

Member of: GSA, GBGSA, IAPS, BSA

St David's challenges you – with excellent results.

The Junior School: ages 3-11, prides itself on its bright, cheerful setting which radiates warmth and care.

In the Senior School: our professional team runs a challenging programme.

GCSE Business studies, Theatre Studies, Technology are there, with three languages, three Sciences and the other essentials totalling 21 subjects.

A level Economics, Government & Politics, Theatre Studies, Psychology and Computer Studies added to the expected range, offer 21 options.

Our Sixth Form is a Consortium with Halliford Boys' School.

Flexi-boarding is an additional service: stay

for prep and supper, or for the week or the term.

Scholarships academic, music, art, sport, particularly gymnastics.

The Most Honourable and Loyal Society of Ancient Britons, a registered charity, aims to provide education for girls to the age of 18 in the buildings and land of the Society at Ashford, Middlesex.

Don't forget to read the articles at the beginning of the book – they may save you a lot of time and trouble

---

MDX

Twickenham Preparatory School

(Founded 1932)

*Beveree, 43 High Street,
Hampton, Middlesex TW12 2SA
Tel: 0181 979 6216*

Head: Mr G D Malcolm, BA
Type: Co-educational Day Preparatory School
Age range: 4-13
No of pupils enrolled as at 6.2.95:
Junior: 24 Boys 42 Girls; Senior: 29 Boys 34 Girls
Fees per annum: £2385-£3810

Religious affiliation: Non-denominational

Member of: IAPS

Twickenham Preparatory School Trust aims to give children a good academic start to their education in a quiet, settled atmosphere in our delightful new surroundings.

Curriculum: Boys are prepared for Common Entrance and Scholarship examinations to Independent Secondary Schools. Girls take entry examinations to local Independent Day Schools at 11.

Music and drama are actively encouraged, as

are many extra-curricular activities. Main team games are Netball, Rounders, Soccer and Cricket which are played on the adjacent sports field. Children are taught to swim.

Entry requirements: Details are set out in our Prospectus.

Twickenham Preparatory School Trust, which is a registered charity, exists to provide a high quality education for local children.

Northamptonshire

Oxfordshire

St Edward's School Oxford

(Founded 1863)

Oxford OX2 7NN
Tel: 01865 319200 Fax: 01865 319202

Head: Mr D Christie, BA, BSc(Econ)
(Member of HMC)
Type: Independent Boarding & Day School
with girls in Sixth Form
Age range: 13-18. Boarders from 13
No. of pupils enrolled as at 1.9.94: 572
Senior: 512 Boys 60 Girls; Sixth Form: 191 Boys 60 Girls
Fees per annum: Day: £8850, Boarding: £11,790

Religious denomination: Church of England

Member of: HMC, GBA, ISCO

Situated on a 90-acre site between town and country the School offers high academic standards combined with a friendly, caring atmosphere and strong traditions in music, drama, art and sport.

There are eight boarding houses with a separate new residence for boarding girls.

Girls and dayboys have studies in the boarding Houses. Each House has a resident Housemaster assisted by several non-resident tutors and a House Nurse.

Recent new facilities include the Design Centre, a Mathematics building (with its own computer network) and an Astroturf all-weather pitch.

Curriculum: The first year is a foundation year, in which boys take the full range of

subjects, including Art and Design and a choice of Greek, German or Spanish. In the two years to GCSE, 10 subjects are studied. There is a wide range of choices within a framework of a balance of Arts, Sciences and Languages. 93% of GCSE grades have been A, B or C.

A good range of A level subjects is available including Social Biology, Politics, Economics, Design, Spanish and German. A pass rate of 95% (with 73% at Grades A, B or C) was obtained in 1992. Over 90% of pupils go on to Higher Education.

Entry: For boys at 13+ by Common Entrance, the Scholarship examination, or our own Assessment Day (for pupils from maintained schools). Up to 15 Scholarships and Exhibitions are available, including awards for Music and Art.

Entry for boys and girls into the Sixth forms is by examination and interview in November. Up to six Scholarships and Exhibitions are available. Sixth form entrants may also enter for the Music Scholarship.

St Edward's School, which is a Charity, exists to provide an excellent all round education for its pupils.

Surrey

SUR

King Edward's School

(Founded 1553)

Witley,
Wormley, Godalming,
Surrey GU8 5SG
Tel: 01428 682572 Fax: 01428 682850

Headmaster: Mr R J Fox, MA, CMath, FIMA
Type: Co-educational Independent School
Age range: 11-18. Boarders from 11
No. of pupils enrolled as at 1.5.95: 505
Junior: 49 Boys 52 Girls
Senior: 110 Boys 101 Girls
Sixth Form: 82 Boys 64 Girls
Fees per term:
Day: £2000; Boarding: £2875

Religious affiliation: Church of England

Member of: HMC, BSA

Curriculum: Art, Biology, Business Studies, Classics, German, English, Economics, French, Geography, History, Latin, Mathematics, Physics, Chemistry, Information Technology, Religious Studies, Drama, CDT, Home Technology, Music.

Entry requirements: Own entrance examination at 11, 12 or 13, or Common Entrance. Good GCSE results and school report for Sixth Form entrance.

King Edward's School, which is a registered charity, provides a structured approach to education and offers a substantial number of bursaries to children whose home circumstances make boarding a real need.

Sussex

WSX

Great Ballard School

(Founded 1924)

*Eartham,
Nr Chichester,
West Sussex PO18 0LR
Tel: 01243 814236 Fax: 01243 814586*

Headmaster: Mr Richard E T Jennings, CertEd
Type: Co-educational Preparatory and
Pre-Preparatory School
Age range: 3-13. Boarders from 7
No. of pupils enrolled as at 1.5.95: 155
Fees per term:
Day: 3-7: £930; ½ Day: £520; 7-13: £1538- £1638
Boarding: £2221-£2321

Religious affiliation: Church of England

Member of: IAPS

Curriculum: The curriculum covers the normal range of subjects and includes Computing, Design Technology, PE, Music, Drama and Current Affairs. Children are prepared for Common Entrance and Scholarship Examinations to appropriate Senior Schools, the particular emphasis being to help each and every child to fulfil their potential.

Entry requirements: Entrance is by interview and testing or through the annual Scholarship in January/February.

Great Ballard: The Pre-prep department in its own walled garden inspires children aged 3-7 to achieve high standards while enjoying their very happy and busy schooldays. Music and movement, drama, PE, swimming, computing and cooking are all introduced in these early years.

The Main School starts at age seven; approximately half of the children board, but there is no compulsion to do so at any stage. Boarding may be done on a full, weekly or occasional basis. We are used to arranging travel for children stationed overseas and ensure that, with outings each weekend, there is life outside the School.

Recent improvements include a new Computer Room, Reference Library, Technology Studio and Junior Laboratory.

At Great Ballard we believe that school must provide a stable, caring environment, a place where children are genuinely happy and are involved in a very wide range of activities, where their interest is constantly being stimulated. Exam results are obviously important, but a happy, busy life in which all achieve their maximum potential, must be the main objective.

Don't forget to read the articles at the beginning of the book – they may save you a lot of time and trouble

WSX

Handcross Park School

(Founded 1887)

*Handcross,
Haywards Heath,
West Sussex RH17 6HF
Tel: 01444 400526 Fax: 01444 400527*

Head: Mr W J Hilton, BA, CertEd
(Member of IAPS)
Type: Independent Co-educational
Weekly Boarding and Day School
Age range: 2½-13. Boarders from 7
No. of pupils enrolled as at 1.9.94:
138 Boys 101 Girls
Fees per term: Day: £1045-£1950
Boarding: £2380

Religious denomination: Church of England

Member of: IAPS

Curriculum: The School maintains high academic standards and prepares children for Public School scholarships and Common Entrance. Handcross Park is a busy school with good musical, artistic and sporting traditions and is situated on a beautiful 57 acre country estate, close to the major (Sussex) towns of Horsham, Crawley and Haywards Heath. Facilities include golf course, new Music School (1987), Nursery, Pre-Preparatory School (1990). (New Sports Hall due 1995).

Entry requirements: By interview with the Headmaster. Scholarship Examinations take place each January/February.

The Newells School Trust Ltd is a Charitable Trust which aims to provide a high quality education for each individual child.

Looking for a school somewhere else in Britain? Why not consult *Which School?* now in its 70th edition, also published by John Catt Educational Ltd

Windlesham House School

(Founded 1837)

Washington,
Pulborough,
West Sussex RH20 4AY
Tel: 01903 873207 Fax: 01903 873017

Heads: Ian and Margaret Angus
Type: Co-educational Boarding School
Age range: 7-13
No. of pupils enrolled as at 1.4.95:
200 Boys 130 Girls
Fees per annum: Boarding: £8460

Religious denomination: Church of England

Ask the children at Windlesham what they like best about their school and their reply will be, almost without exception, the very wide range of activities available here. Ask the children's parents what makes Windlesham such a very special school and they would probably say its strong family feeling and the knowledge that the children's happiness and care come at the top of our list of priorities.

We are an all boarding prep school with a long and well established history of being in the forefront of educational development: creativity and innovation abounds. One of Windlesham's great strengths is that we genuinely offer a co-educational environment and have done for more than 25 years. The number of boys and girls here is very well balanced. The boys and girls do all classes and activities together which it is sensible for them to share. Our curriculum is very broad and this, together with our talented and creative staff, enables us to place great emphasis on the individual development of each child, academically, socially and emotionally. By offering such a wide ranging programme of study we aim to give our children an opportunity to discover where their individual talents lie and then teach them to use those talents to the full. We feel that the confidence gained from doing something really well, whatever it may be, is easily transferred to other areas of life and learning.

Our academic standards are high and we

gain numerous scholarships to senior schools each year. We are also able to give special help and support to those with specific learning difficulties. We have a teacher pupil ratio of 1:9 and our average class size is 17. We teach all the subjects required by the Common Entrance board plus Latin. Those who wish can do Greek. In addition on the timetable you will find Spanish, Art and Pottery, Design and Technology, Drama, Music, Physical Education and Games. We place strong emphasis on the use of computers here and our two computer rooms are always full whether it is lesson time or free time.

We have excellent facilities: a beautiful theatre which converts easily to an open space for sport plus two more halls for games, gymnastics and dance, a chapel, libraries, two science laboratories, a music school, art and pottery rooms, a design centre, two squash courts, eight tennis courts, indoor swimming pool and extensive playing fields.

Our week-end arrangements are flexible. We do not have fixed week-end exeats as many of our children's parents work abroad. It is a rare week-end when we have less than 100 children here, enjoying our fun and busy week-end programme which we see as a very important part of our offering. Those going out at week-ends leave after Saturday morning lessons at 12 noon and return by seven o'clock on Sunday evenings. We now run a weekly bus from Putney on Sunday evenings. We are very experienced at making arrangments to transfer to the major airports children who need to travel on international airlines at half-term and the end of term.

The Malden Trust Ltd, which is a Charitable Trust, exists to provide high quality boarding education for boys and girls between the ages of 7 and 13 years.

SUS

Worth School

(Founded 1933)

Worth Abbey,
Turners Hill, Nr Crawley,
Sussex RH10 4SD
Tel: 01342 715911

Headmaster: The Rev P C Jamison, MA(Oxon)
Type: Boys' Independent Boarding and Day School
Age range: 9-18
No of pupils enrolled as at 1.2.95:
(9-13) 68; (13-18) 297
Average size of class: 18 (GCSE) 12 (A level)
Teacher/Pupil ratio: 1:8
Fees per term: Junior House £1825-£2735;
Senior House £2470-£3700

Religious affiliation: Predominantly Roman Catholic

Member of: HMC, BSA, SHA

Curriculum: Nine subjects are taken at GCSE, and boys normally take three at A levels, out of a choice of 18. The A level pass rate is over 90%. Almost all leavers go on to university, with 10% gaining admission to Oxford or Cambridge.

Entry requirements: Entry to the Junior House (at aged 9+) is via the School's own Assessment Test. Entry to the Senior School (at aged 13+) is via the Common Entrance exam, in which we require an average of 50%. Sixth Form places at age 16+ are also available.

Scholarships/Bursaries available: Seven or

eight academic awards ranging in value from 15% to 50% of the annual fees; up to six Music Scholarships/Bursaries; also a number of Sixth Form Scholarships.

Facilities: Currently IT is being developed in a unique fashion, with three network rooms, and up to 200 computers being installed over the next three years. There is a full range of games and activities, including a six-hole Golf course. Voluntary Service and the Duke of Edinburgh's Award Scheme are strongly supported. There is a plethora of Clubs/Societies and we encourage boys to involve themselves in a wide range of extra-curricular activities, especially music and drama.

As a Benedictine School, Worth tries to help its pupils to achieve excellence in this world and salvation in the next.

Worth is a Charitable Trust (Charity No 233572).

Wales

WAL

Howell's School

(Founded 1860)

Cardiff Road,
Llandaff, Cardiff,
South Glamorgan CF5 2YD
Tel: 01222 562019 Fax: 01222 578879

Head: Mrs C J Fitz, BSc
Member of GSA, SHA, GPDST
Type: Girls Independent School
Age range: 4-18
No. of pupils enrolled as at 1.9.94: 685
Junior: 131; Senior: 421; Sixth Form: 133
Fees per annum:
Day and Sixth Form Day: £3804; Junior: £2808

Religious denomination: Non-denominational

Member of: GSA, GPDST

Curriculum: In the Junior School all National Curriculum subjects including Welsh are taught. Many subjects are thematically linked and cross curricular. In the Senior School years 7-9 follow a broad and balanced curriculum and all National Curriculum subjects are studied, plus Latin and German. At GCSE the girls follow a core of English, French, Mathematics and Double Award Science, with many other subjects on offer. At A and AS level the girls are able to choose from a large group which meet individual requirements.

Entry requirements: Entry to the school at 4+, 11+ and 16+. Enquiries to the Admissions Secretary in the Autumn Term for the following September.

Howell's School is a registered charity which exists to provide high quality education for local girls.

WAL

Haberdashers' Monmouth School for Girls

(Founded 1892)

*Hereford Road,
Monmouth, Gwent NP5 3XT
Tel: 01600 714214*

Head: Mrs D L Newman, BA(Hons)English,
PGCE(London)
Type: Independent Girls' School
Age range: 7-18. Boarders from 7-18
No of pupils enrolled as at 1.9.94: 646
Junior: 92 Senior: 403 Sixth Form: 151
Fees per annum:
Day: £1092-£1332; Boarding: £2514
Sixth Form: Day £1450; Boarding £2632

Religious affiliation: Christian Foundation

Member of: GSA

Curriculum: The curriculum is designed to avoid specialisation at too early an age. Academic standards are high and the very wide curriculum is guided by, but not limited to, the National Curriculum. Girls are extremely successful in gaining places at Oxford and Cambridge and the majority of leavers go on to university.

Entry requirements: Entry by examination at 11, 13 and post GCSE. Tests for entry to the Preparatory School are held in the Spring term.

The Haberdashers' Monmouth School for Girls, which is a registered charity, exists to provide and conduct a day and boarding school in Monmouth.

Directory of Tutorial Colleges and Colleges of Further Education

American Colleges in the UK

UNDERWOOD COLLEGE
See Business & Secretarial section.

Art, Fine Art, and Photography

HARTON MANOR SCHOOL OF FURNITURE MAKING
See Other Specialist section.

SYMONDSBURY MANOR TUTORIAL COLLEGE
See GCE A-Level/GCSE Independent Tutorial Colleges section.

THE TOTNES SCHOOL OF GUITARMAKING
See Other Specialist section.

Business & Secretarial

BOURNEMOUTH COMPUTER AND TECHNOLOGY CENTRE
See Computer, Electronics, Specialist section.

MLS INTERNATIONAL COLLEGE
8 Verulam Place, Bournemouth, Dorset BH1 1DW
Tel: (01202) 291556
Head: Mr B Henwood

PAMELA NEAVE TRAINING CENTRE
18 St Augustines Parade, Bristol, Avon BS1 4UL
Tel: (0117) 9211831
Head: Mrs J Derrick-Smith

SWIFT TRAINING CENTRE
187 Queen Street, Newton Abbot, Devon
Tel: (01626) 65284
Head: R Flemming

UNDERWOOD COLLEGE
Glen Fern Road, Bournemouth, Dorset BH1 2LU
Tel: (01202) 552624
Head: A Yeadon

Computer, Electronics, Specialist

BOURNEMOUTH COMPUTER AND TECHNOLOGY CENTRE
63 Cavendish Road, Bournemouth, Dorset BH1 1RA
Tel: (01202) 290943
Head: Ruth Marsden

PAMELA NEAVE TRAINING CENTRE
See Business & Secretarial section.

UNDERWOOD COLLEGE
See Business & Secretarial section.

Cookery & Home Economics

COOKERY AT THE GRANGE
The Grange, Whatley Vineyard, Frome, Somerset BA11 3LA
Tel: (01373) 836579
Head: Miss J Crosswell-Jones

GCE A-Level/GCSE Independent Tutorial Colleges

BRIDGE TUTORIAL COLLEGE
3 Bennett Street, Bath, Avon BA1 2QQ
Tel: (01225) 465453
Head: Mrs Lara Brown

CENTRAL COLLEGE FOR SIXTH FORM STUDIES
17 Gandy Street, Exeter, Devon EX4 3LS
Tel: (01392) 436708
Head: Miss J P Ward

CLIFTON TUTORS
31 Pembroke Road, Clifton, Bristol, Avon BS8 3BE
Tel: (0117) 973 8376
Head: W P Shaw

MANDER PORTMAN WOODWARD
10 Elmdale Road, Clifton, Bristol, Avon BS8 1SL
Tel: (0117) 925 5688
Head: Ms F A Eldridge

PLYMOUTH TUTORIAL COLLEGE (EGAS)
11 Seaton Avenue, Mutley, Plymouth, Devon PL4 6QJ
Tel: (01752) 261229
Head: Mr Stoyel & Mrs Stoyel

SYMONDSBURY MANOR TUTORIAL COLLEGE
Symondsbury, Bridport, Dorset DT6 6HD
Tel: (01308) 456288
Head: P W Hitchin

THE TUTORIAL COLLEGE
44/46 Magdalen Road, Exeter, Devon EX2 4TE
Tel: (01392) 78101
Head: K D Jack

Interior Design and Restoration

THE TOTNES SCHOOL OF GUITARMAKING
See Other Specialist section.

Music

THE TOTNES SCHOOL OF GUITARMAKING
See Other Specialist section.

Other Specialist

HARTON MANOR SCHOOL OF FURNITURE MAKING
Harton Manor, Hartland, Bideford, Devon EX39 6BL
Tel: (01237) 441288
Head: D Charlesworth

PRODIVE LTD
Services Area, Falmouth Docks, Cornwall TR11 4NR
Tel: (01326) 315691
Head: Mr E J Wills

THE TOTNES SCHOOL OF GUITARMAKING
Collins Road, Totnes, Devon TQ9 5PJ
Tel: (01803) 865255
Head: N Reed

Display Listings of Tutorial Colleges and Colleges of Further Education in areas outside the South West

London

FE

The Arts Educational London Schools

(Founded 1919)

*Cone Ripman House,
14 Bath Road,
Chiswick, London W4 1LY
Tel: 0181 994 9366 Fax: 0181 994 9274*

Principal: Mr Peter Fowler, MA, FTCL, LRAM,
ARAM, FRSA (Member of CDET, ISAI)
Type: Independent Co-educational Day School
Age range: 16-19
No. of students enrolled as at 1.5.95: 128
30 Boys 98 Girls
Fees per annum:
Dance School: £6705
Musical Theatre School: £7047

Religious affiliation: Non-denominational

Accredited by the Council for Dance Education and Training

Courses offered: 3-year Dance Course – thorough training in Ballet, Contemporary, Repertoire, Jazz and Tap.
3-year Musical Theatre Course – specialist training in Dance, Drama, Voice and Singing as an integrated course. Tuition is given in lectures, classes, small groups, one-to-one, portfolio courses, plus A levels in Dance,

Drama and Theatre Arts (as part of Foundation Drama Course) and English.

Superbly appointed premises in Chiswick include fully equipped proscenium arch theatre, studio theatre, spacious practice rooms and rehearsal facilities.

The Arts Educational Schools Trust, a registered charity, exists to train students and pupils in academic studies and the performing arts of the theatre.

Inchbald
School of Design

(Founded 1960)

Interior Design Faculty

7 Eaton Gate, London SW1W 9BA
Tel: 0171 730 5508 Fax: 0171 730 4937

**Garden Design Faculty and
Design History Faculty**

32 Eccleston Square, London SW1V 1PB
Tel: 0171 630 9011 Fax: 0171 976 5979

Principal: Mrs Jacqueline Duncan, ISID, IDDA
No. of students enrolled as at 1.5.94:
Male 15 Female 105
Range of fees (including VAT): from £8900
Other courses (from 3-day to 10-week):
range from £520 to £3250

Diploma Courses:
Environmental Design (3-year; 2-year)
Interior Design (2-year; 1-year; 1-year with
Advanced Studies)
Garden Design (1-year)
Design History (1-year)

Certificate Courses:
Design & Decoration (10-week)
Design History (3 x 10-week)
Garden Design (3 x 10-week)
Design & Drawing Foundation (6-week)

Short Courses: Selection varying in length
from 3-day to 3-week courses in interior
design, design history, garden design,

computer aided design, colour, business
management for designers, design drawing,
design of furniture and built-in fitments, and
decorative paint finishes.

Nature of tuition: Lectures, classes, small
groups, one-to-one, practical projects and
visits.

Average class or group: 20

Teacher/Student ratio: 1: 8

The School provides an assistance service for
accommodation. A non-residential adult
education school situated in Belgravia and
Pimlico with excellent access to London
museums, exhibitions and leading designers.

**A list of useful Educational Associations
appears at the back of this book**

WH

Leith's School of Food & Wine

(Founded 1975)

21 St Alban's Grove,
London W8 5BP
Tel: 0171 229 0177 Fax: 0171 937 5257

Principals: Caroline Waldegrave; Fiona Burrell
Type: Non Residential Tertiary Education
Age range: 18-40
No of pupils enrolled as at 1.5.95:
18 Boys 78 Girls
Fees per annum: £8000

Leith's School of Food and Wine opened in 1975, to provide professional training for career cooks and short courses for enthusiastic amateurs. The guiding principle of the teaching at Leith's is to impart enthusiasm for the trade and instil a lasting love of good food and wine in the students. There is a commitment to classical techniques and methods, but with a fresh modern approach. Students leave having acquired all the essential skills and confidence necessary to be a success.

The School has 96 full time students with a purpose built demonstration theatre and excellent teaching kitchens. The School provides a Diploma course and four Certificate courses, all with examinations. These qualifications are well recognised in the catering business and career opportunities include hotels and restaurants, chalet cooking, freelance work, television, recipe-writing, food styling or working in the wine trade. The School holds Career seminars, provides advice and gives training in interview techniques.

Holiday, evening, part-time and specialist courses provide scope for interested amateurs.

Leith's many cook books, published by Bloomsbury are produced at the school. Moet and Chandon and Mouton Cadet sponsor prestigious awards for Diploma students.

The School is owned by Caroline Waldegrave and Sir Christopher Bland. It has close links

with Leith's catering business and Leith's Restaurant.

The School has an employment agency 'Leith's List' which is in constant touch with cooks and employers.

All courses are open to adults of either sex. The School is non-residential but students are helped to find local accommodation, if necessary.

Examinations offered: Leith's Diploma in Food & Wine; Leith's Beginners/ Intermediate/Advanced Certificate in Food & Wine; Leith's Basic Certificate in Practical Cookery.

Mander Portman Woodward

(Founded 1973)

108 Cromwell Road,
London SW7 4ES
Tel: 0171 835 1355 Fax: 0171 259 2705

Heads: Dr Nigel Stout, MA, DPhil
Miss Fiona Dowding, MA
Type: Independent Fifth and Sixth Form College
Age range: 15-18+
No of pupils enrolled as at 1.5.95: 329
GCSE Level: 25 Boys 15 Girls
A Level: 168 Boys   121 Girls
Fees per term: Fees are charged per course:
GCSE (6 subjects) £2730; A Level (3 subjects): £2763

Member of: CIFE, BAC, DFE

MPW is a co-educational college in South Kensington. One and two year courses and short re-take courses are offered in a wide range of A Level and GCSE subjects. Preparation is given for Oxford and Cambridge Entrance. Facilities include four Science laboratories, computer room, Art and Pottery studios, library and reading rooms and a student cafe. Teaching takes place in small classes of seven or fewer. Individual tuition is also available by arrangement. Each student has a Personal Tutor to monitor progress and give advice on higher education and employment opportunities.

Educational Associations

Educational Associations

The Allied Schools
Provision of financial services and advice to member schools (Stowe School, Wrekin College, Canford School, Harrogate Ladies' College, Westonbirt School, Felixstowe College, Riddlesworth Hall School) and of secretariat for the Governing Bodies of those schools.
General Manager, David Harris,
42 South Bar Street, Banbury,
Oxon OX16 9XL
(01295 256441)

The Association of British Riding Schools
An independent body of proprietors and principals of riding establishments, aiming to look after their interests and those of the riding public, to raise standards of management, instruction and animal welfare.
General Secretary,
Association of British Riding Schools,
Old Brewery Yard, Penzance,
Cornwall TR18 2SL
(01736 69440)

The Association of Heads of Independent Schools
Membership is open to all Heads of Girls' and Co-Educational Junior Independent Schools which are accredited by the ISJC (Independent Schools Joint Council).
Honorary Secretary: Mrs J Kingsley MA,
Abbot's Hill School, Bunkers Lane,
Hemel Hempstead,
Hertfordshire HP3 8RP

The Association of Nursery Training Colleges
For information on Careers in Child Care, Careers as Nannies, Careers as Nursery Workers and on NVQ in Child Care and Education offered in the three independent Nursery Training Colleges, please contact:
Norland College,
Denford Park, Hungerford,
Berks RG17 0PQ
(01488 682252)

The Association of Tutors Incorporated
This Association is the professional body to further the interests of tutors. Members include tutors teaching every academic and vocational subject at all levels of education, including tutorial college principals.
Enquiries to: Dr D J Cornelius, PhD, BSc,
Sunnycroft, 63 King Edward Road,
Northampton NN1 5LY
(01604 24171)

The Boarding Schools Association
The BSA is concerned that boarding education remains a healthy and relevant resource readily available to all who need it, within the range of educational provision in this country.
Secretary: F Bickerstaff JP, BSc,
Westmorland, 43 Raglan Road,
Reigate,
Surrey RH2 0DU

British Association for Commercial and Industrial Education
A member organisation concerned with all aspects of vocational education and training. Further information from:
The Librarian,
British Association for Commercial and Industrial Education,
35 Harbour Exchange Square,
London E14 9GE
(0171 987 8989)

The British Association for Early Childhood Education
A Charitable Association prepared to give advice on matters concerned with the care and education of young children from birth to nine years. Publishes booklets and organises conferences for those interested in Early Years Education.
The Secretary, BAECE Headquarters,
111 City View House, 463 Bethnal Green Road,
London E2 9QY
(0171 739 7594)

The Choir Schools Association
Schools which educate Cathedral and Collegiate choristers.
Administrator: R J Shephard,
The Minster School
Deangate, York YO1 2JA
(01904 625217)

Common Entrance Examinations

Details of the Common Entrance Examinations, which provide standard entrance papers for boys and girls transferring from junior to senior schools at 11+, 12+ and 13+ are available from The Administrator at the address below. Copies of syllabuses and past papers are obtainable from CE Publications Ltd at the same address. Tel No 01425 610016

Common Entrance Board,
Jordan House, Christchurch Road,
New Milton, Hants BH25 6QJ
(01425 621111 Fax: 01425 620044)

CIFE
(Conference for Independent Further Education)

CIFE is the professional association for independent sixth form and tutorial colleges accredited by the British Accreditation Council for Independent Further and Higher Education or the Independent Schools Joint Council. Colleges seeking to be accredited by either body within three years can be admitted to candidate membership. Member colleges specialise in preparing students (mainly over statutory school-leaving age) for GCSE and A and A/S Level examinations and for university entrance. The aim of the association is to provide a forum for the exchange of information and ideas, and for the promotion of best practice, and to safeguard adherence to strict standards of professional conduct and ethical propriety. Information published by member colleges as to their exam results is subject to regulation and to validation by Gabbitas Educational Consultants as academic auditor to CIFE. Further information from:

Myles Glover MA,
Buckhall Farm, Bull Lane,
Bethersden, near Ashford,
Kent TN26 3HB
(01233 820 797)

The Dyslexia Institute Ltd

A registered, educational charity which has established teaching, assessment and teacher-training centres throughout England. The aim of these Institutes is to help dyslexics of all ages to overcome their difficulties in learning to read, write and spell and to achieve their potential. (Leaflets supplied with SAE).

Information Officer:
The Dyslexia Institute Head Office,
133 Gresham Road,
Staines TW18 2AJ
(01784 463851)

The Governing Bodies Association & The Governing Bodies of Girls Schools Association
The objects of the Association are to advance education in Independent Schools, to discuss matters concerning the policy and administration of Independent Schools, and to encourage co-operation between their governing bodies.
Enquiries to: D G Banwell, BA,
Windleshaw Lodge,
Withyham, near Hartfield,
East Sussex TN7 4DB
(01892 770879)

Girls' Schools Association

130 Regent Road, Leicester LE1 7PG
(Tel: 0116 254 1619 Fax: 0116 255 3792)
President: Mrs Penelope Penney
General Secretary: Ms Sheila Cooper

The Girls' Schools Association exists to represent the 240 schools whose Heads are in membership. Its direct aim is to promote excellence in the education of girls. This is achieved through a clear understanding of the individual potential of girls and young women. Over 110,000 pupils are educated in schools which cover day and boarding, large and small, city and country, academically elite and broad based education.
Scholarships, bursaries and Assisted Places are available in most schools.

The Girls Public Day School Trust

26 Queen Anne's Gate,
London SW1H 9AN
Tel: 0171 222 9595
The Trust was founded in 1872 and was a pioneer of education for girls. Today the pupils in its 26 independent schools (listed below) number over 18,500.

BATH HIGH SCHOOL, Hope House, Lansdown, Bath BA1 5ES
BIRKENHEAD HIGH SCHOOL, 86 Devonshire Place, Birkenhead, Merseyside L43 1TY
BLACKHEATH HIGH SCHOOL, Vanbrugh Park, London SE3 7AG

BRIGHTON AND HOVE HIGH SCHOOL, The Temple, Montpelier Road, Brighton, Sussex BN1 3AT

BROMLEY HIGH SCHOOL, Blackbrook Lane, Bickley, Bromley, Kent BR1 2TW

CHARTERS-ANCASTER, Penland Road, Bexhill-on-Sea, E Sussex TN4 02JQ

CROYDON HIGH SCHOOL, Old Farleigh Road, Selsdon, South Croydon CR2 8YB

HEATHFIELD SCHOOL, Beaulieu Drive, Pinner, Middlesex HA5 1NB

HOWELLS SCHOOL, Llandaff, Cardiff CF5 2YD

IPSWICH HIGH SCHOOL, Woolverstone Hall, Ipswich, Suffolk IP4 2UH

KENSINGTON PREPARATORY SCHOOL FOR GIRLS, 17 Upper Phillimore Gardens, London W8 7HF

LIVERPOOL: THE BELVEDERE SCHOOL, 17 Belvidere Road, Princes Park, Liverpool L8 3TF

NEWCASTLE: CENTRAL NEWCASTLE HIGH SCHOOL, Eskdale Terrace, Newcastle upon Tyne NE2 4DS

NORWICH HIGH SCHOOL, 95 Newmarket Road, Norwich, Norfolk NR2 2HU

NOTTINGHAM HIGH SCHOOL FOR GIRLS, 9 Arboretum Street, Nottingham NG1 4JB

NOTTING HILL & EALING HIGH SCHOOL, 2 Cleveland Road, Ealing, London W13 8AX

OXFORD HIGH SCHOOL, Belbroughton Road, Oxford OX2 6XA

PORTSMOUTH HIGH SCHOOL, Kent Road, Southsea, Hampshire PO5 3EQ

PUTNEY HIGH SCHOOL, 35 Putney Hill, London SW15 6BH

SHEFFIELD HIGH SCHOOL, 10 Rutland Park, Sheffield S10 2PE

SHREWSBURY HIGH SCHOOL, 32 Town Walls, Shrewsbury, Shropshire SY1 1TN

SOUTH HAMPSTEAD HIGH SCHOOL, 3 Maresfield Gardens, London NW3 5SS

STREATHAM HILL & CLAPHAM HIGH SCHOOL, Abbotswood Road, London SW16 1AW

SUTTON HIGH SCHOOL, 55 Cheam Road, Sutton, Surrey SM2 2AX

SYDENHAM HIGH SCHOOL, 19 Westwood Hill, London SE26 6BL

WIMBLEDON HIGH SCHOOL, Mansel Road, London SW19 4AB

The schools are not denominational. Entry is by interview and test appropriate to the pupil's age.

All schools have a Junior Department. Kensington is a preparatory school only. Charters-Ancaster has boarding facilities.

The schools participate in the Government's Assisted Places Scheme, offering places at 11+ and at Sixth Form level (except Heathfield and Charters-Ancaster).

For further details please contact the schools direct, or there is a general prospectus available from the GPDST office giving the addresses of all the schools, together with the current fees, and other general information.

The Girls Public Day School Trust is a charity Reg. No. 1026057 which exists to provide high quality education.

The Headmasters' Conference
Membership (239) consists of Heads of major boys' and co-educational independent schools. The objects of the annual meeting are to discuss matters of common interest to members.
Membership Secretary:
R N P Griffiths,
1 Russell House,
Bepton Road, Midhurst,
West Sussex, GU29 9NB
Secretary:
V S Anthony
130 Regent Road,
Leicester LE1 7PG

The Incorporated Association of Preparatory Schools
IAPS is the professional association of headmasters and headmistresses of preparatory schools in the UK and overseas. Membership is open to suitably qualified heads and deputy heads accredited by the Independent Schools Joint Council. Further information from:
The General Secretary:
John Morris,
11 Waterloo Place,
Leamington Spa,
Warwickshire CV32 5LA
(01926 887833)

Independent Beauty Schools Association
The functions of the Association are to help maintain high standards of training in the member schools; to liaise with examining boards; to be represented on the Health and Beauty Therapy Training Board. Please write for a list of member schools and a copy of
A Guide to Training In Beauty Therapy.
PO Box 781,
London SW3 2PN

Independent Business Training Association

IBTA has been established as an association of the leading private business and secretarial colleges with the objective of promoting the highest possible standards of commercial training in the UK. The Association also offers a free advisory service to prospective students to help them select a suitable course and College of study.

Miss O Edwards,
IBTA,
24 Queensberry Place,
South Kensington,
London SW7 2DS

The Independent Schools Association Incorporated

Membership is limited to the Heads of Schools which are not under the direct control of the Department for Education. The Association aims to co-operate with other bodies which stand for professional freedom in education and to maintain for Independent Schools due recognition by government and the general public of their place in the educational life of the nation.

Secretary: Timothy Ham, MA, DipEd,
Boys' British School,
East Street, Saffron Walden,
Essex CB10 1LS
(01799 523619)

The Independent Schools Bursars' Association

Membership: 600 independent secondary schools. Objectives include promotion of administrative efficiency and exchange of information between member schools.

Secretary: D J Bird,
Woodlands, Closewood Road,
Denmead, Waterlooville,
Hants PO7 6JD
(01705 264506)

The Independent Schools Careers Organisation

The organisation's objects are: to assist careers staff in schools, to assist employers in making career opportunities and qualifications known, to advise children and their parents on careers, higher education and opportunities available, and to arrange courses for staff and pupils.

Administrative Director,
The Independent Schools Careers Organisation,
12a Princess Way,
Camberley,
Surrey GU15 3SP
(01276 21188 Fax: 01276 691833)

The Independent Schools Information Service
Established by the leading Associations of Independent Schools to provide information about schools to parents and the media.
Director: D J Woodhead,
ISIS National Headquarters,
56 Buckingham Gate,
London SW1E 6AG
(0171 630 8793/4)

The Independent Schools Joint Council
The ISJC considers matters of policy and administration common to its members and when required speaks collectively on their behalf. It represents its constituent members in joint discussions with the. Department for Education and with other organisations.

ISJC is a federation of the following associations:

Governing Bodies Association   (GBA)
Governing Bodies of Girls' Schools Associations (GBGSA)
Headmasters' Conference   (HMC)
Girls' Schools Association   (GSA)
Society of Headmasters and Headmistresses of
    Independent Schools   (SHMIS)
Incorporated Association of Preparatory Schools (IAPS)
Independent Schools' Association Incorporated (ISAI)
Independent Schools Bursars' Association (ISBA)

Their combined membership comprises about 1,400 schools.

General Secretary: Dr Arthur Hearnden OBE,
Grosvenor Gardens House,
35-37 Grosvenor Gardens,
London SW1W 7BS
(0171 630 0144 Fax: 0171 931 0036)

The Montessori Training Organisation
Affiliated to the Association Montessori Internationale. Further information from:
The Secretary,
The Maria Montessori Training Organisation,
26 Lyndhurst Gardens,
Hampstead,
London NW3 5NW
(0171 435 3646)

The Round Square Schools

An international group of schools following the principles of Kurt Hahn, the founder of Salem School in Germany, and Gordonstoun in Scotland was formed in 1967. The Round Square Conference, named after Gordonstoun's 17th century circular building in the centre of the school, now has 25 member schools in nine countries: Australia, Canada, England, Germany, India, Kenya, Scotland, Switzerland and the United States.

Member schools arrange regular exchange visits for pupils and undertake aid projects in India, Kenya, Venezuela and Eastern Europe. All schools in the Conference uphold the five principles of outdoor adventure, community service, education for democracy, international understanding and environmental conservation.

The member schools in the United Kingdom are:

GIRLS	CO-EDUCATIONAL
Cobham Hall, Kent	Abbotsholme, Derbyshire
St Anne's, Cumbria	Box Hill, Surrey
Westfield, Newcastle upon Tyne	Gordonstoun, Scotland
	Rannoch, Scotland

For more information about Round Square Schools, please contact:
Kay Holland, Secretary
Round Square Conference
Box Hill School,
Dorking, Surrey RH5 6EA
(01372 377812)

The Secondary Heads Association

An association representing the majority of Heads and Deputy Heads in all types of secondary schools and colleges.
General Secretary: J Sutton, MA, FRSA, FIMgt
130 Regent Road,
Leicester LE1 7PG
(0116 247 1797 Fax: 0116 247 1152)

The Society of Headmasters and Headmistresses of Independent Schools

A society of some 70 schools, most of which have a strong boarding element.
Honorary Secretary: A E R Dodds, MA,
Mantons,
Park Road,
Winchester,
Hampshire SO23 7BE
(01962 862579 Fax: 01962 878981)

Steiner Fellowship

Representing Rudolf Steiner Waldorf Education in the UK and Eire. The 26 schools affiliated to the Fellowship are to be distinguished from the curative homes and schools, also based on the work of Steiner, which are for emotionally disturbed and handicapped children.

The Secretary,
Steiner Schools Fellowship,
Kidbrooke Park,
Forest Row,
Sussex RH18 5JB
(01342 822115 Fax: 01342 826004)

WES - World-Wide Education Service, Home School

The WES Home School Service enables parents to teach their own children at home, either overseas or in the UK. Full courses of study or single subjects to support local schooling are available for children aged 3-12 years. All courses are consistent with the National Curriculum. For further information contact:

The World-Wide Education Service,
35 Belgrave Square,
London SW1X 8QB
(0171 235 2880 Fax: 0171 259 5234)

World-Wide Education Service Ltd

The objectives of the service, which was established over a century ago, are (1) to provide full professional support to overseas British and International Schools which includes inspection, in-service teacher training, curriculum and management advice, feasibility studies and setting up new schools; (2) to undertake OFSTED UK inspections at both primary and Secondary level and to offer advice and support to UK Schools, particularly to 'clustered' groups; (3) recruitment of teaching staff to overseas schools.

WES World-wide Education Service,
Canada House,
272 Field End Road,
Eastcote,
Middlesex HA4 9NA
(0181 866 4400 Fax: 0181 429 4838)

The Woodard Schools

In 1848 Nathaniel Woodard founded Lancing College and by 1891, when he died, had established seven schools. The Woodard Corporation now has 36 schools throughout the country, including 11 Associated schools. All have an Anglican foundation and together form the largest group of Church Schools in England and Wales. Further information from:

The Registrar,
The Woodard Schools,
1 The Sanctuary, Westminster,
London SW1P 3JT
(0171 222 5381)

THE SOUTH-WEST

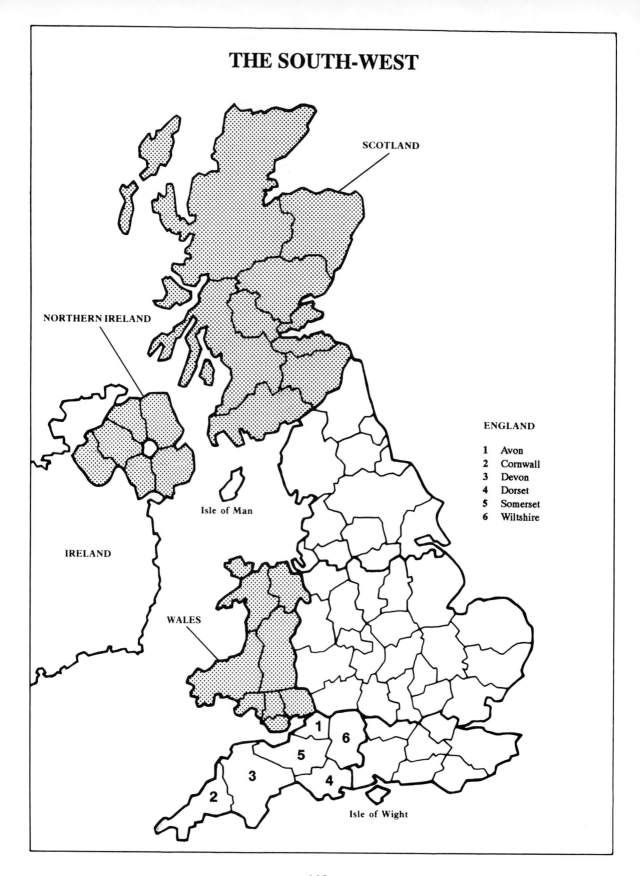

SCOTLAND

NORTHERN IRELAND

IRELAND

Isle of Man

WALES

ENGLAND

1 Avon
2 Cornwall
3 Devon
4 Dorset
5 Somerset
6 Wiltshire

Isle of Wight

Index

A

Abbey School, Glastonbury D36
All Hallows, Shepton Mallet D36
Allhallows School, Lyme Regis D33
Amberley House School, Bristol D24
The Arts Educational London Schools, London W4 101
Ashbrooke House, Weston-Super-Mare D26

B

Badminton School, Bristol D24, 43
Bath High School GPDST, Bath D24
Beehive School, Taunton D36
Bendarroch School, Exeter D29
Blundell's School, Tiverton D32
Bournemouth Computer and Technology Centre,
    Bournemouth D98
Bramdean Grammar School, Exeter D29
Bramdean Preparatory & Grammar School, Exeter D29
Breaside Preparatory School, Bromley 77
Bredon School, near Tewkesbury 72
Bridge Tutorial College, Bath D98
Bristol Cathedral School, Bristol D25
Bristol Grammar School, Bristol D25, 44
Bristol Waldorf School, Bristol D25
Bruton School for Girls, Bruton D35
Bryanston School, Blandford Forum D32
Buckholme Towers, Poole D34
Buckland School, Watchet D37

C

Calder House School, Nr Bath D38, 58
Canford School, Wimborne D35
Castle Court Preparatory School, Wimborne D35
Central College for Sixth Form Studies, Exeter D98
Chafyn Grove School, Salisbury D38
Chard Independent School, Chard D35
Cheam Hawtreys School, Newbury D69
Chilton Cantelo School, Yeovil D37
Claysemore Preparatory School, Blandford Forum D32
Claysemore School, Blandford Forum D32
Cleve House School, Bristol D25
Clifton College Preparatory School, Bristol D25
Clifton College, Bristol D25
Clifton High School, Bristol D25, 45
Clifton Lodge, London W5 .... 65, 79
Clifton Tutors, Bristol D98
Colston's Collegiate School, Bristol D25
Colston's Girls' School, Bristol D25

Cookery at the Grange, Frome D98
Croft House School, Blandford Forum D32

D

Dauntsey's School, Devizes D38
Dorchester Preparatory School, Dorchester D33
Downside School, Bath D24
Duke of York's Royal Military School, Dover 78
Dumpton School, Wimborne D35

E

Edgarley Hall (Millfield Junior School), Glastonbury D36, 56
Edgehill College, Bideford D28
Elm Grove School, Exeter D29
Emanuel School, London SW11 80
Exeter Cathedral School, Exeter D29
Exeter Preparatory School, Exeter D29
Exeter School, Exeter D29

F

Fairfield PNEU School, Bristol D25
Falcon Manor, Towcester 88
Flambeaux Montessori School/Day Nursery, Salisbury D38
Fletewood School, Plymouth D31

G

Gracefield Preparatory School, Bristol D25
Gramercy Hall School, Brixham D29
Great Ballard School, Nr Chichester 91
Grenville College, Bideford D29
Greylands School, Paignton D30
Grittleton House School, Chippenham D38

H

Haberdashers' Monmouth School for Girls, Monmouth 96
Handcross Park School, Haywards Heath 92
Hanford School, Blandford Forum D32
Harton Manor School of Furniture Making, Bideford D98
Heywood Preparatory School, Corsham D38
Homefield School (Preparatory), Bournemouth D33
Homefield School, Christchurch D33
Howell's School, Cardiff 95
Hylton Kindergarten & Pre-preparatory School, Exeter D29

I

Inchbald School of Design, London SW1 102
International School of London, London W3 81

K

Kelly College Junior School - St Michael's, Tavistock D31
Kelly College, Tavistock D31
King Edward's Junior School, Bath D24
King Edward's School, Bath, Bath D24
King Edward's School, Godalming 90
King's Bruton Pre-Preparatory & Junior School, Yeovil D37
King's College, Taunton D36
King's Hall School, Taunton D36
King's School, Bruton D35
King's School, Plymouth D31
Kingsbridge Preparatory School, Kingsbridge D30
Kingsbury Hill House, Marlborough D38
Kingswood Day Preparatory School, Bath D24
Kingswood School, Bath D24
Knighton House, Blandford Forum D32

L

L'Ecole des Petits, London SW6 82
La Retraite Leehurst School, Salisbury D39
Lancaster House School, Weston-Super-Mare D26
Lanherne School, Dawlish D29
Leaden Hall School, Salisbury D39, 59
Leith's School of Food & Wine, London W8 103
Lord Wandsworth College, Hook 74

M

Mander Portman Woodward, Bristol D98
Mander Portman Woodward, London SW7 104
Manor House School, Honiton D30
Marlborough College, Marlborough D38, 60
Millfield School, Street D36
Milton Abbey School, Blandford Forum D32
Miss Morleys' Nursery School, SW1 84
MLS International College, Bournemouth D98
Monkton Combe Junior School, Bath D24
Monkton Combe School, Bath D24
The Montessori House, London N10 83
Motcombe Grange School, Shaftesbury D34
Mount House School, Tavistock D31
Mount St Mary's Convent School, Exeter D30, 48

N

Newell House School, Sherborne D34
Northaw School, Salisbury D39

O

Oak Hill School, Bristol D25
Overndale School, Bristol D25

P

Pamela Neave Training Centre, Bristol D98
Pangbourne College, Near Reading 70
Paragon School, Bath D24
Perrott Hill School, Crewkerne D35, 57
Pinewood School, Swindon D39, 61
Plymouth College Preparatory School, Plymouth D31
Plymouth College, Plymouth D31
Plymouth Tutorial College (EGAS), Plymouth D98
Polwhele House School, Truro D28
Port Regis, Shaftesbury D34
Prior Park College, Bath D24
Prior Park Preparatory School, Swindon D39
Prodive Ltd, Falmouth Docks D98

Q

Quantock School, Bridgwater D35
Queen Anne's School, Reading 71
Queen Elizabeth's Hospital, Bristol D26
Queen's College Junior School, Taunton D36
Queen's College, Taunton D36

R

Redland High School for Girls, Bristol 46
Redland High School, Bristol D26
Roselyon School, Par D27
Rossholme School, Highbridge D36
Rudolf Steiner School, Totnes D32
Rydal Pre-preparatory School, Clevedon D26

S

Sacred Heart Preparatory School, Bristol D26
Salisbury Cathedral School, Salisbury D39, 62
Sandroyd, Salisbury D39, 62
Sands School, Ashburton D28, 49
Selwyn School, Gloucester 73
Shebbear College, Beaworthy D28
Sherborne Preparatory School, Sherborne D34, 55
Sherborne School for Girls, Sherborne D21, D34
Sherborne School, Sherborne D34
Shobrooke House School, Crediton D29
Sidcot School, Winscombe D27, D37, 57
Silverhill School, Bristol D26
Sinclair House School, London SW6 85
Small School, Bideford D29
St Andrew School, Marlborough D38
St Antony's-Leweston Preparatory School, Sherborne D34

St Antony's-Leweston Preparatory School, Sherborne ..D34, 54
St Antony's-Leweston School, Sherborne D34, 53
St Aubyns School, Tiverton D32
St Bernard's Preparatory School, Newton Abbot D30
St Bernard's School, Newton Abbot 50
St Brandon's School, Clevedon D26
St Christopher School, Letchworth 76
St Christopher's, Burnham-on-Sea D35
St David's College, West Wickham 78
St David's School, Ashford 86
St Dunstan's Abbey Preparatory School, Plymouth D31
St Dunstan's Abbey School, Plymouth D31
St Edward's School, Oxford 89
St Genevieve's School, Dorchester D33
St John's School, Sidmouth D31
St Joseph's Convent Nursery School, Poole D34
St Joseph's School, Launceston D27
St Margaret's Exeter, Exeter D30
St Martin's Independent School, Crewkerne D36
St Martin's School, Bournemouth D33
St Mary's School, Calne D38
St Mary's School, Shaftesbury D34
St Michael's School, Barnstaple D28, 51
St Monica's School, Poole D34
St Peter's School, Exmouth D30
St Petroc's School, Bude D27
St Ronan's, Bridport D33
St Swithun's School, Winchester 74
St Thomas Garnet's School, Bournemouth D33
St Ursula's High School, Bristol D26
St Wilfrid's School, Exeter D30
Stonar School, Melksham D38
Stoodley Knowle Convent School, Torquay D32
Stourbridge House School, Warminster D39
Stover School, Newton Abbot D30
Stroud School, Romsey 75
Sunninghill Preparatory School, Dorchester D33
Swan School for Boys, Salisbury D39
Swift Training Centre, Newton Abbot D98
Sydenham High School GPDST, London SE26 86
Symondsbury Manor Tutorial College, Bridport D98

T

Talbot Heath, Bournemouth D33
Talbot House Preparatory School, Bournemouth D33
Taunton Preparatory School, Taunton D36
Taunton School, Taunton D36
The Abbey School, Torquay D32
The Dolphin School, Exmouth D30
The Downs School, Bristol D25
The Duchy Grammar School, Truro D28

The Godolphin School, Salisbury D39
The Hall School (Pre-preparatory for Sidcot School),
    Winscombe D27, 46
The International School of Choueifat, Chippenham D38
The Maynard School, Exeter D30
The Mill School, Devizes D38
The Old Malthouse, Swanage D34
The Park School, Bath D24
The Park School, Bournemouth D33
The Park School, Yeovil D37
The Red Maids' School, Bristol D26
The Royal School, Bath D24, 47
The Royal School, Hampstead, London NW3 84
The School of St Clare, Penzance D28
The Totnes School of Guitarmaking, Totnes D98
The Tutorial College, Exeter D98
Thornlow Junior School, Weymouth D35
Thornlow School, Weymouth D55
Thornlow Senior School, Weymouth D35
Tockington Manor, Bristol D26
Torwood House School, Bristol D26
Tower House School, Paignton D30
Treliske School, Truro D28
Tremore Christian School, Bodmin D27
Tremough Convent School, Penryn D27
Trescol Vean School, Truro D28
Trinity School, Teignmouth D31, 52
Truro High School, Truro D28
Truro School, Truro D28
Twickenham Preparatory School, Hampton 87

U

Underwood College, Bournemouth D98
Uplands School, Poole D34

W

Warminster School, Warminster D39
Wellington School, Wellington D37
Wells Cathedral Junior School, Wells D37
Wells Cathedral School, Wells D37
Wentworth Milton Mount, Bournemouth D33
West Buckland Preparatory School, Barnstaple D28
West Buckland School, Barnstaple D28
Western College Preparatory School, Plymouth D31
Westwing School, Bristol D26
Whitehouse School, Seaton D31
Windlesham House School, Pulburgh 93
Wolborough Hill School, Newton Abbot D30
Worth School, Nr Crawley 94
Wyncroft, Weston-Super-Mare D26